Alicia's Pin-Ups

SCI-FI, FANTASY, & GIRLICIOUS PIN-UP ART

The Art of

Alicia Hollinger

First Printing, 2013

Wonderland Art
ISBN-13: 978-0615871141
ISBN-10: 0615871143

www.WonderlandArt.biz
Facebook: www.Facebook.com/AliciaHollingerArt
Twittter: @AliciaHollinger

FORWARD

So, if you had asked me when I was six what I wanted to be when I grew up, the last thing I would have thought of is "Pin-Up Artist." Not that I even knew what one was, but I remember "Actress" and "Ballerina" as being at the top of the list, although my dancing skills would have Nigel Lythgoe suddenly turn into Simon Cowell on a bad day. But the tutus were cute, all pink and pouffy, and acting, well, I think every little girl wants to be an actress/model at some point, right? But I also liked drawing, especially paper dolls, each with different hair, clothes, and in my mind, a personality that later became part of the drama I created with my collection of paper doll actors. I liked creating people. Maybe what I really wanted to be is a god.

I've heard somewhere (Oprah?) that those who are happiest in life make a living doing something related to what they enjoyed doing most as a child. But now, instead of creating cute paper dolls, I bring into being digital hot girls—fully computer generated people. No photographs of people are used. I combine 3D modeling, digital painting, and an arsenal of digital art tools along with either an over-caffeinated or somewhat dreamy state of mind.

But why half-naked pin-ups, you may ask? Well I started out doing high-fashion looks and then realized there's really not a market for computer-generated models in fashion because there are so many actual living ones who have to wear real life clothes… And then, one day, back in 2009, someone saw my art and suggested I go to Comic-Con in San Diego. "What's that?" I asked. It ended up being something that changed my life. I went into Comic-Con day one, a jaded Hollywood/New York self-professed over-educated party-girl to, after four days of immersion in this strange new land, I emerged—a geek! While standing in a ridiculous line in front of a mock-up of a Stargate from Stargate SG-1 (which I had just started watching the year the series ended and went into syndication) waiting with all the other Stargate fans, something happened. The years of jadedness began to lift and while staring into the epicenter of that Stargate mock-up, feeling almost as if I were in line to go through an actual wormhole, I felt a sudden affinity with those around me. I suddenly GOT IT, I understood geekdom! It wasn't about those nerds in school who covered their work during tests in fear you may copy off them, it was about embracing otherworldly possibilities and immersing yourself in imaginary universes with imaginary people who are beyond mere mortals.

So, it was right there at the Stargate booth at Comic-Con that my whole life changed. I started embracing geekdom. My favorite TV shows became "Stargate SG-1," "Battlestar Galactica," "Firefly," "Eureka," and then "Continuum," and my motto came to be the SYFY Channel's corporate slogan "Imagine Greater."

Oh, and sex sells, so therefore, the scantily clad girls LOL…

So, basically, I drank of the Comic-Con Kool-Aid, and mixed it with my existing Hollywood world of parties filled with Playboy and Maxim models and it turned into the sci-fi, fantasy and "girlicious" pin-ups of today… :) Please follow me on Facebook and Twitter for more art!

XOXO Alicia Hollinger
Facebook: www.facebook.com/AliciaHollingerArt
Twitter: @AliciaHollinger

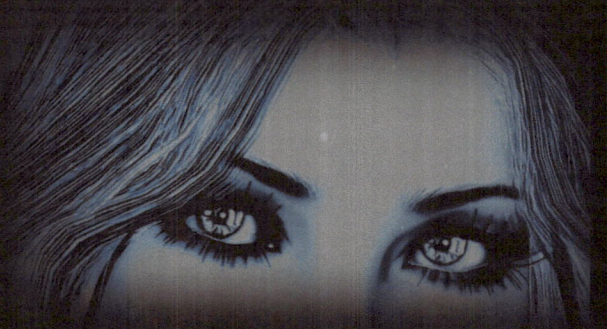

YOU REMEMBER IT, DON'T YOU?

THAT ELUSIVE INCREDIBLE EUPHORIA.

YOU'VE HAD A FLEETING GLIMPSE, MAYBE AS A CHILD, MOST DEFINITELY IN A DREAM. YOU HAVE DEEP-SEATED MEMORIES OF SOMETHING, SOMEWHERE, SOME OTHER PLACE, SOME OTHERWORLDLY PLACE WHERE YOU CAN FLY, MAYBE YOU CAN FEEL COLORS AND MUSIC. WONDERLAND, NEVER-NEVER LAND, OVER THE RAINBOW, THROUGH A WORMHOLE OR STARGATE..? ARTISTS AND WRITERS HAVE TRIED TO DEPICT IT THROUGHOUT THE AGES.

YOU KNOW IT'S THERE AND JUST A BLINK AWAY. IT'S AN INTANGIBLE PLACE WHERE THE COLORS ARE MORE VIBRANT, THERE ARE COLORS THAT DON'T EXIST HERE ON EARTH, IN THIS FREQUENCY WE CALL "REALITY."

ESCAPE FOR A WHILE INTO ANOTHER REALITY.

HAVE A FUN RIDE.

0100000101101100011010010110001101 1
0100101100001001000000100 1000011011
110110110001101100011010010110111 00
1100111011001010111 0010

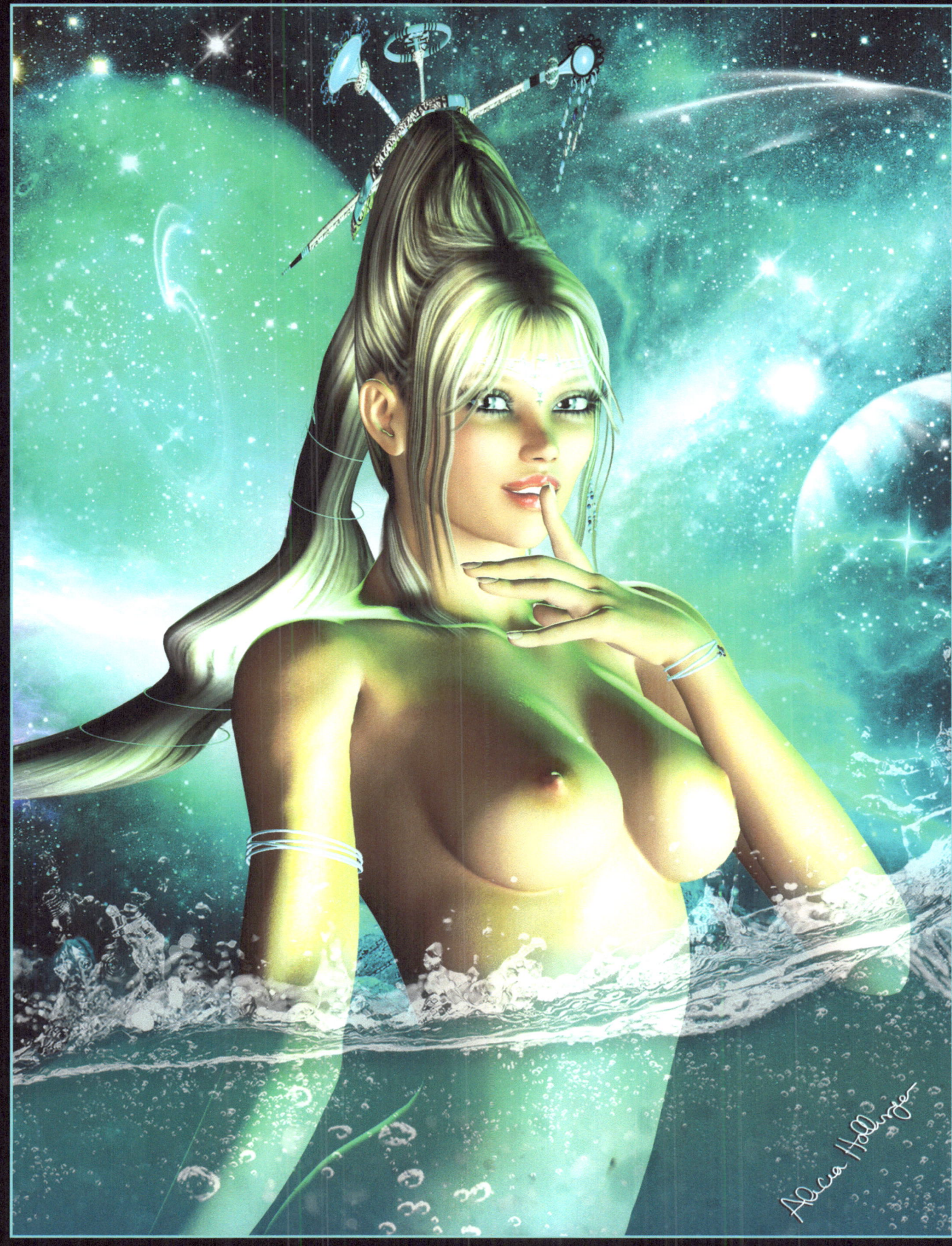

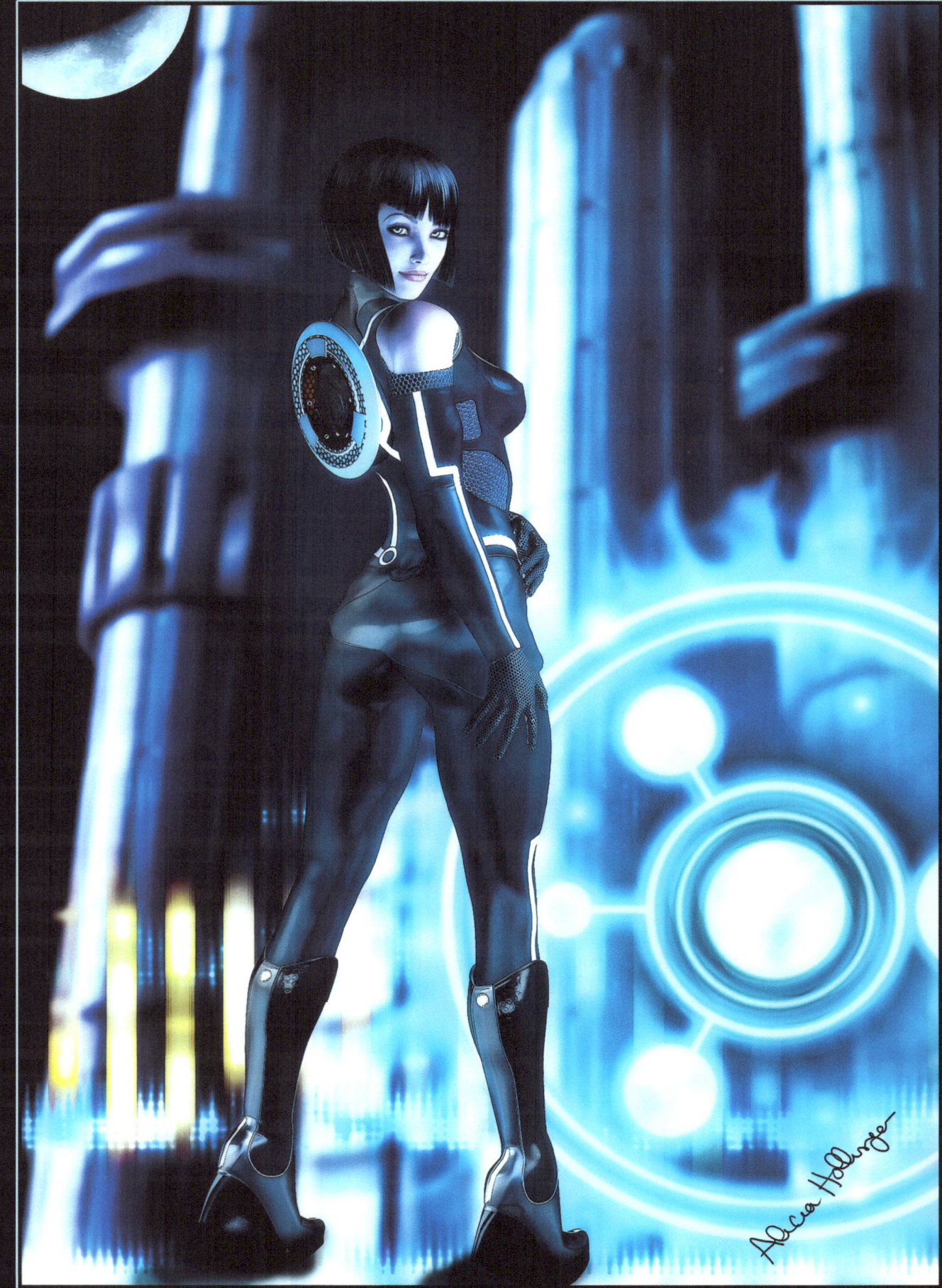

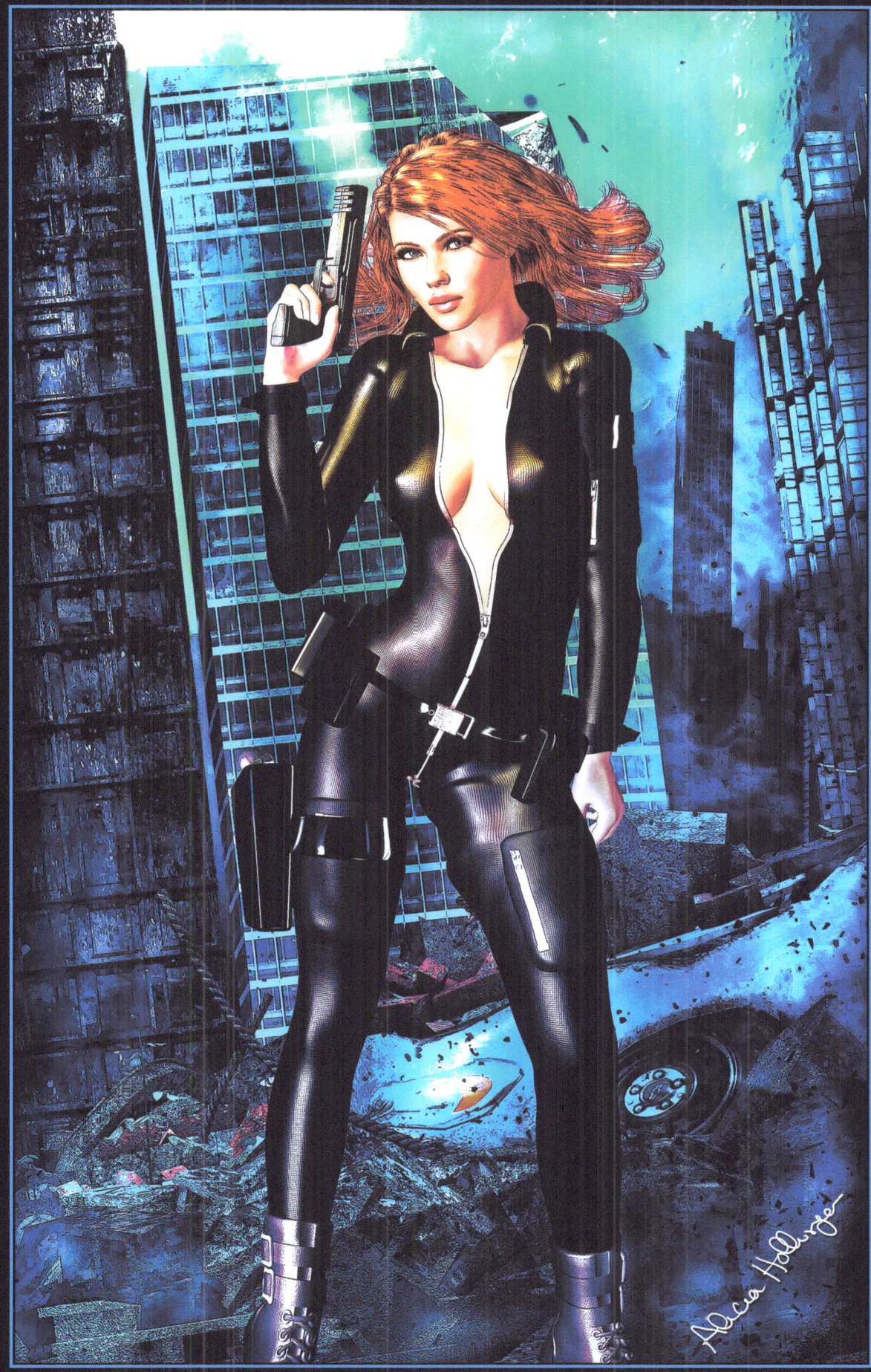

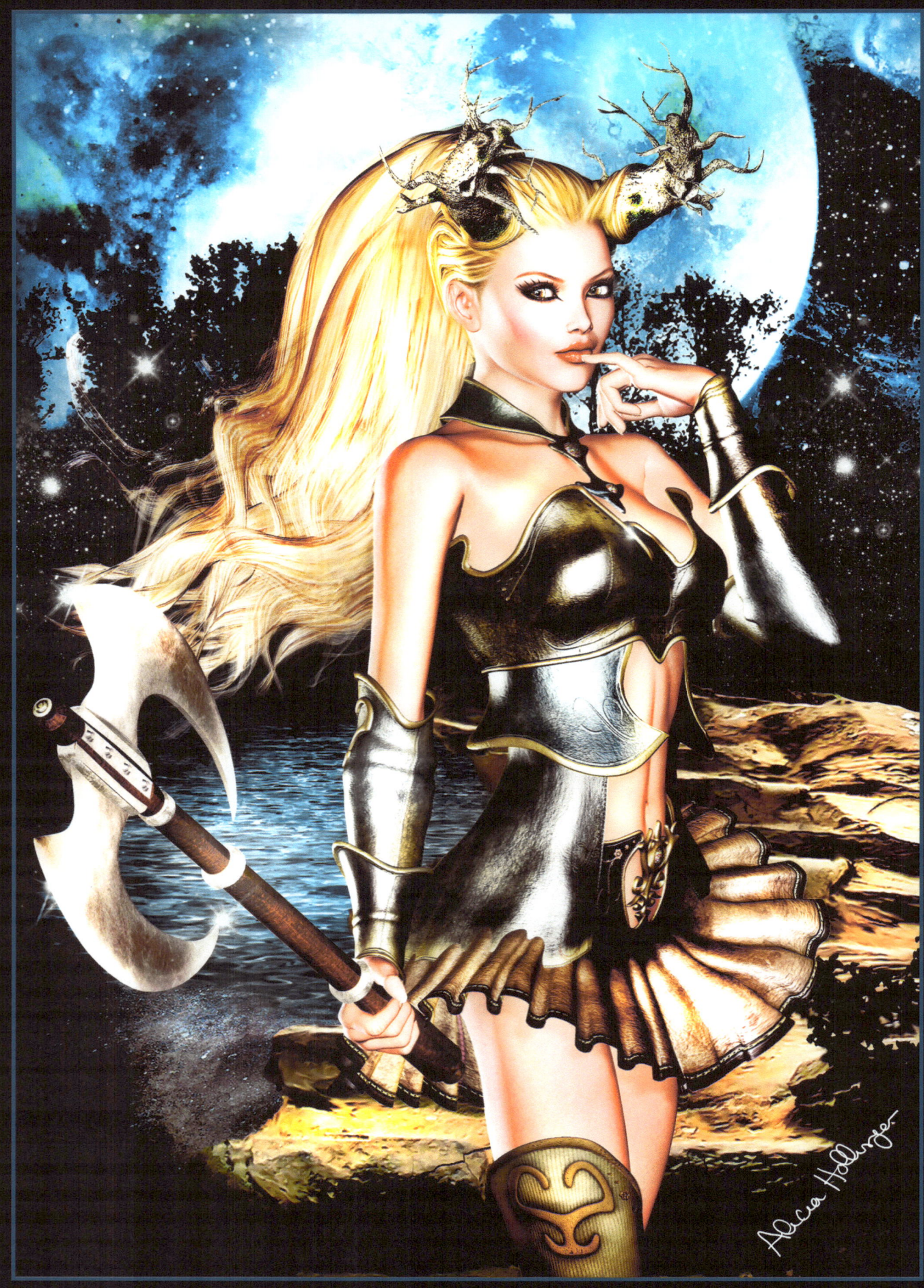

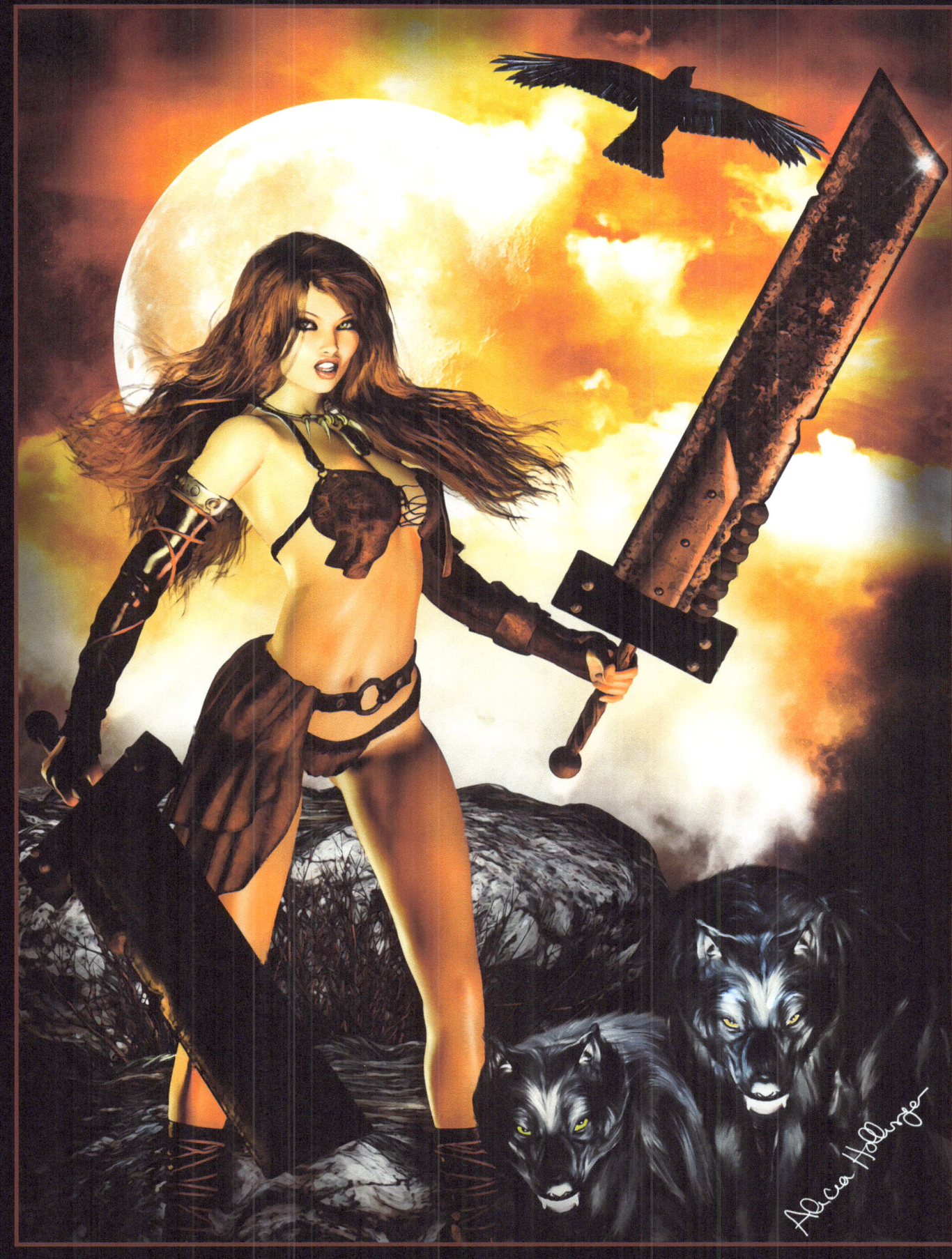

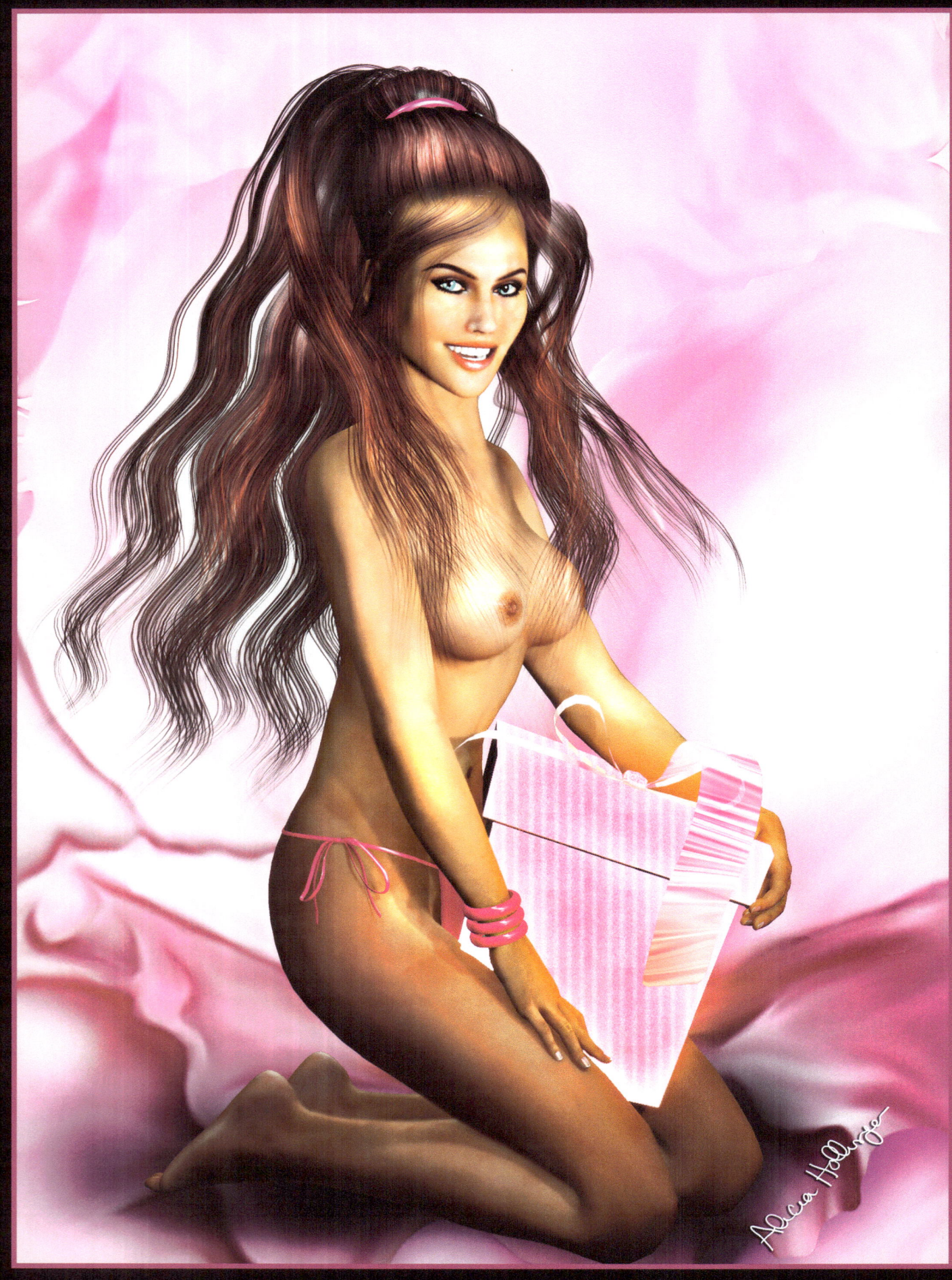

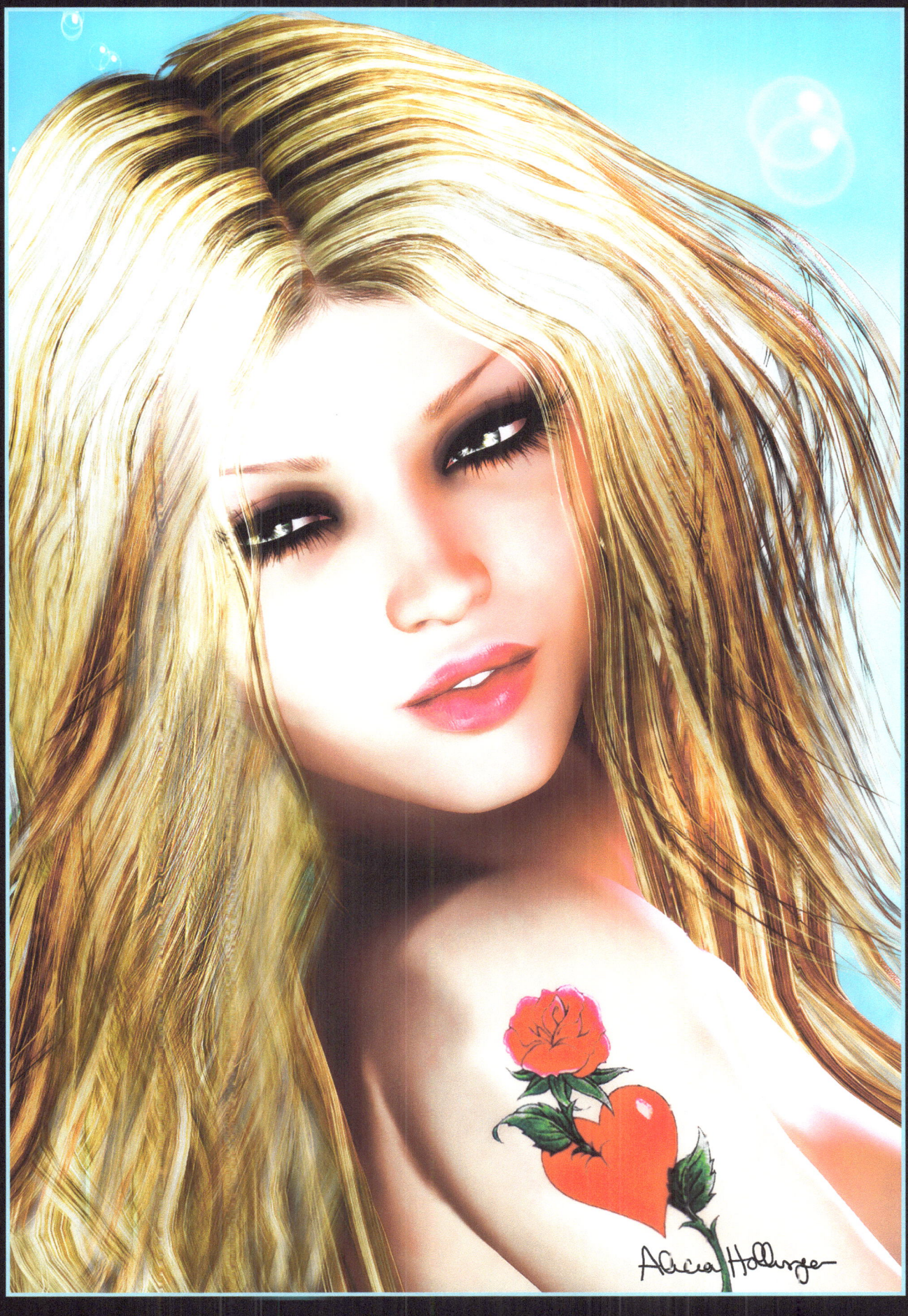

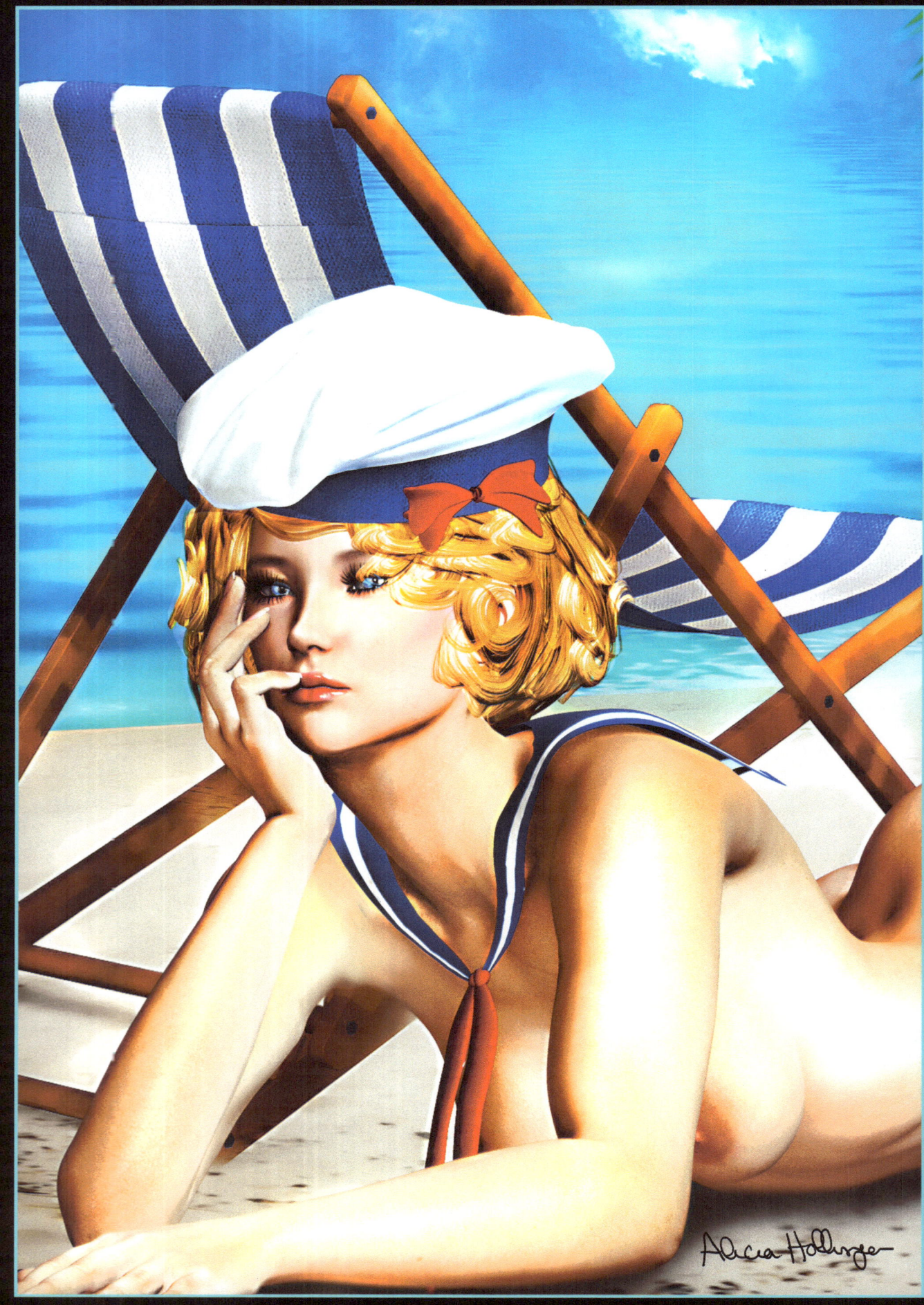

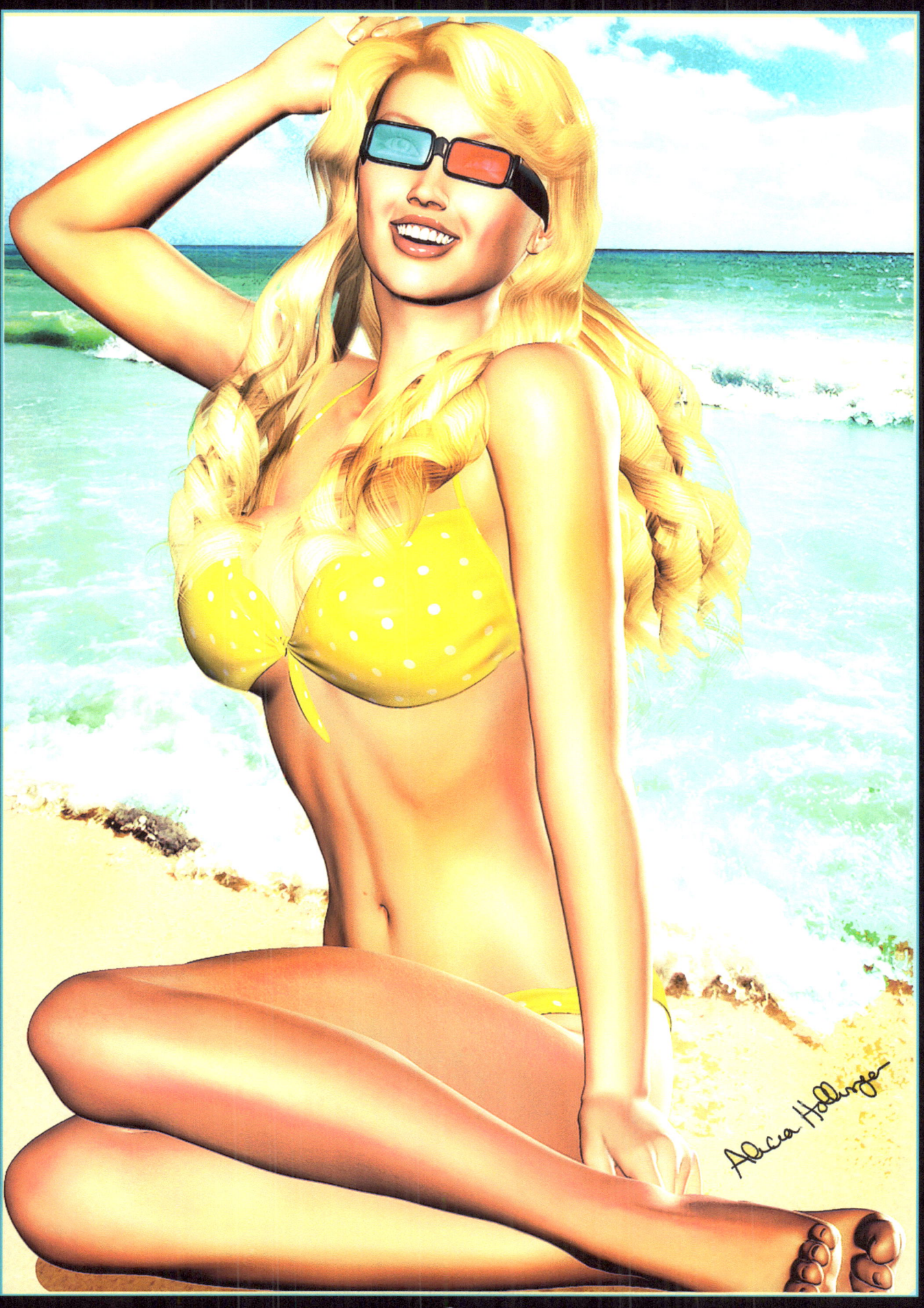

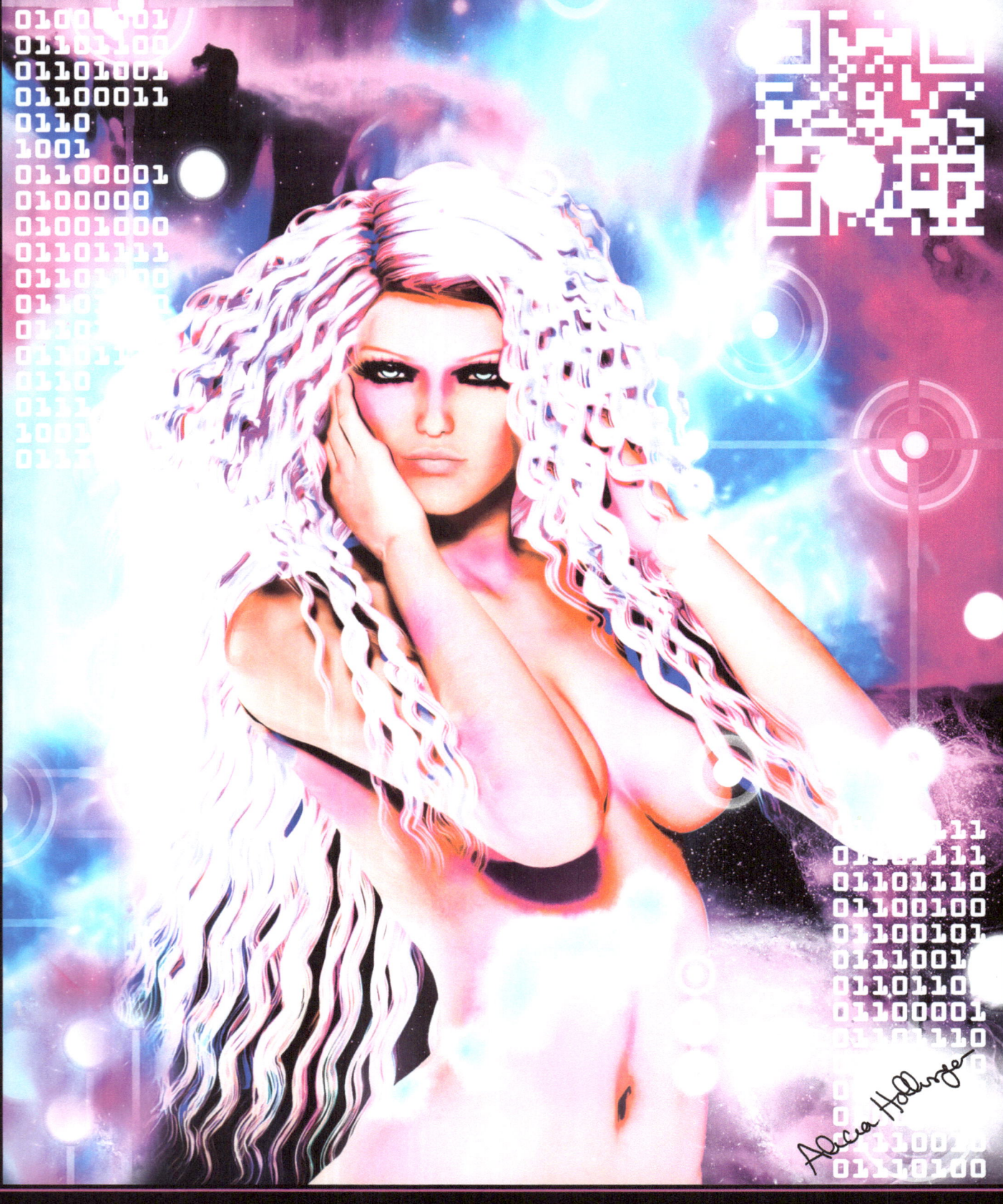

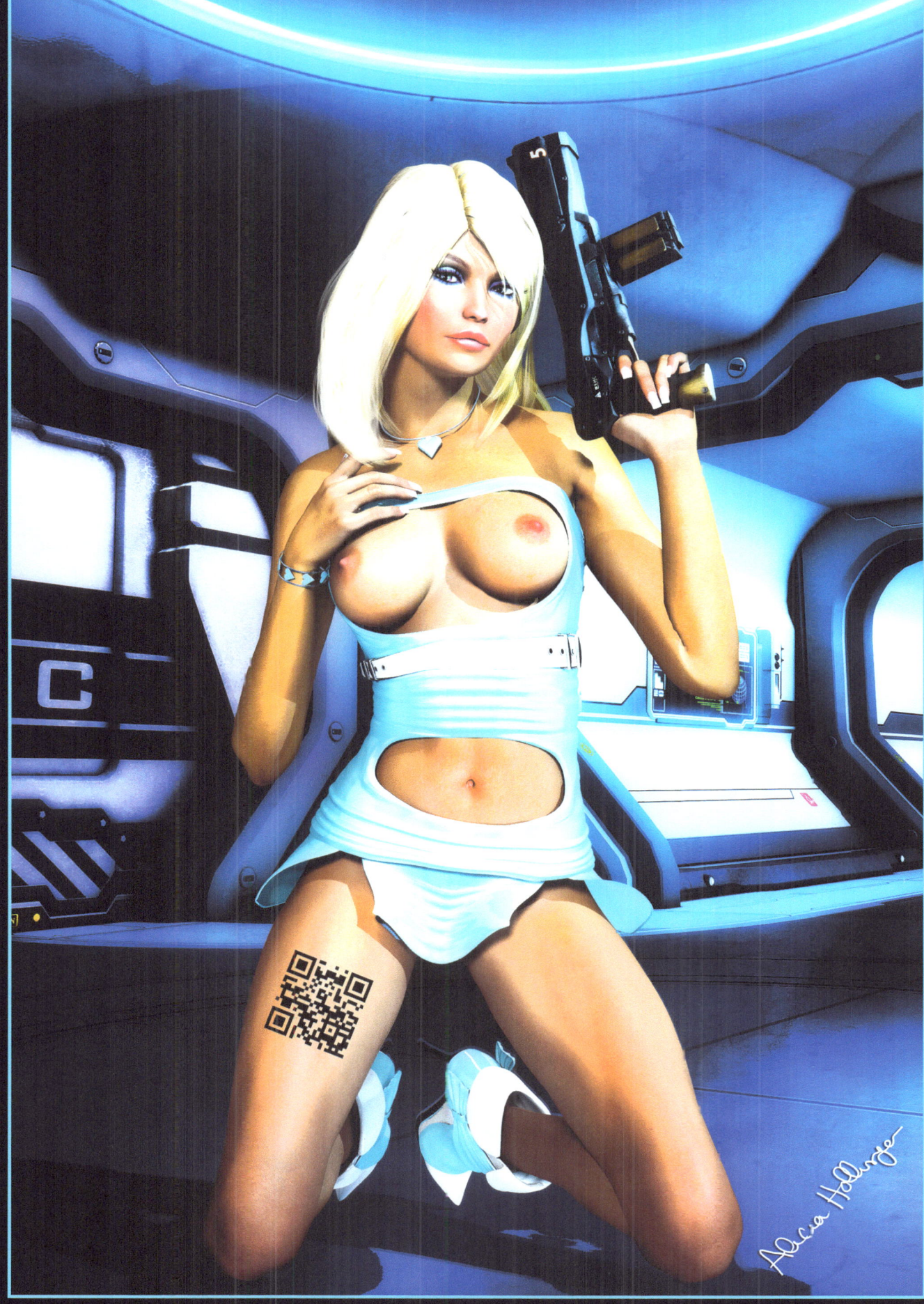

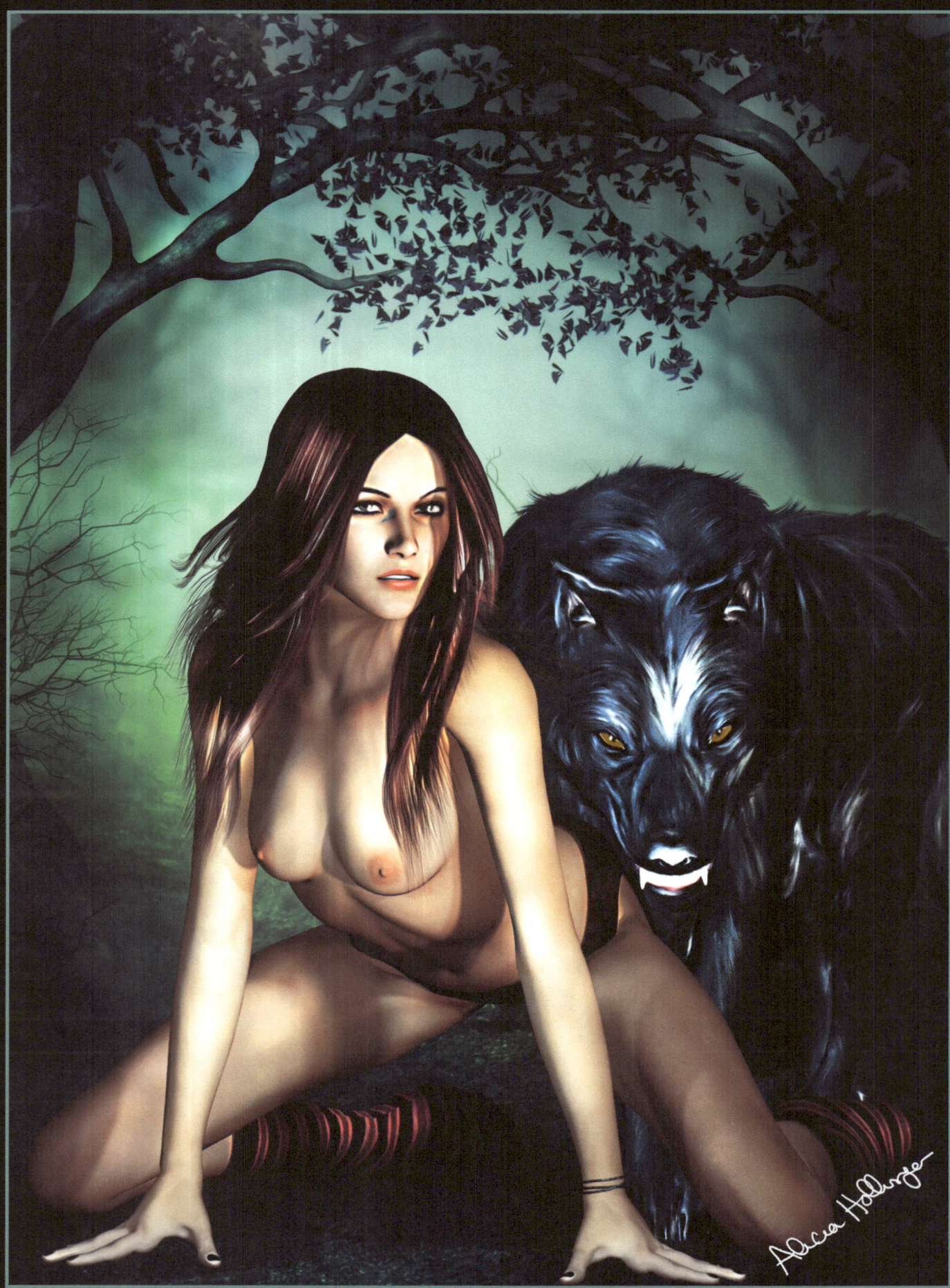

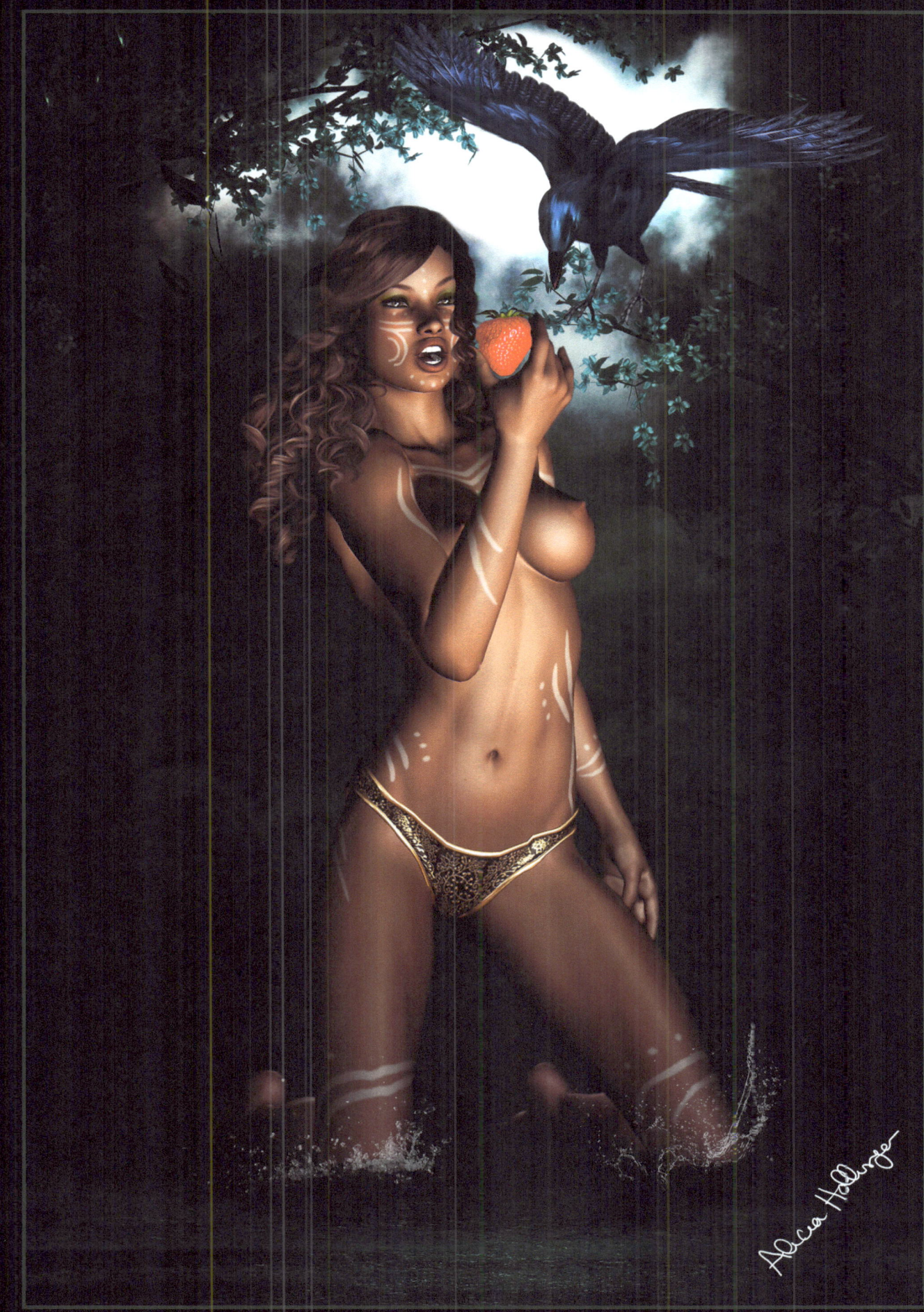

Alicia Hollinger

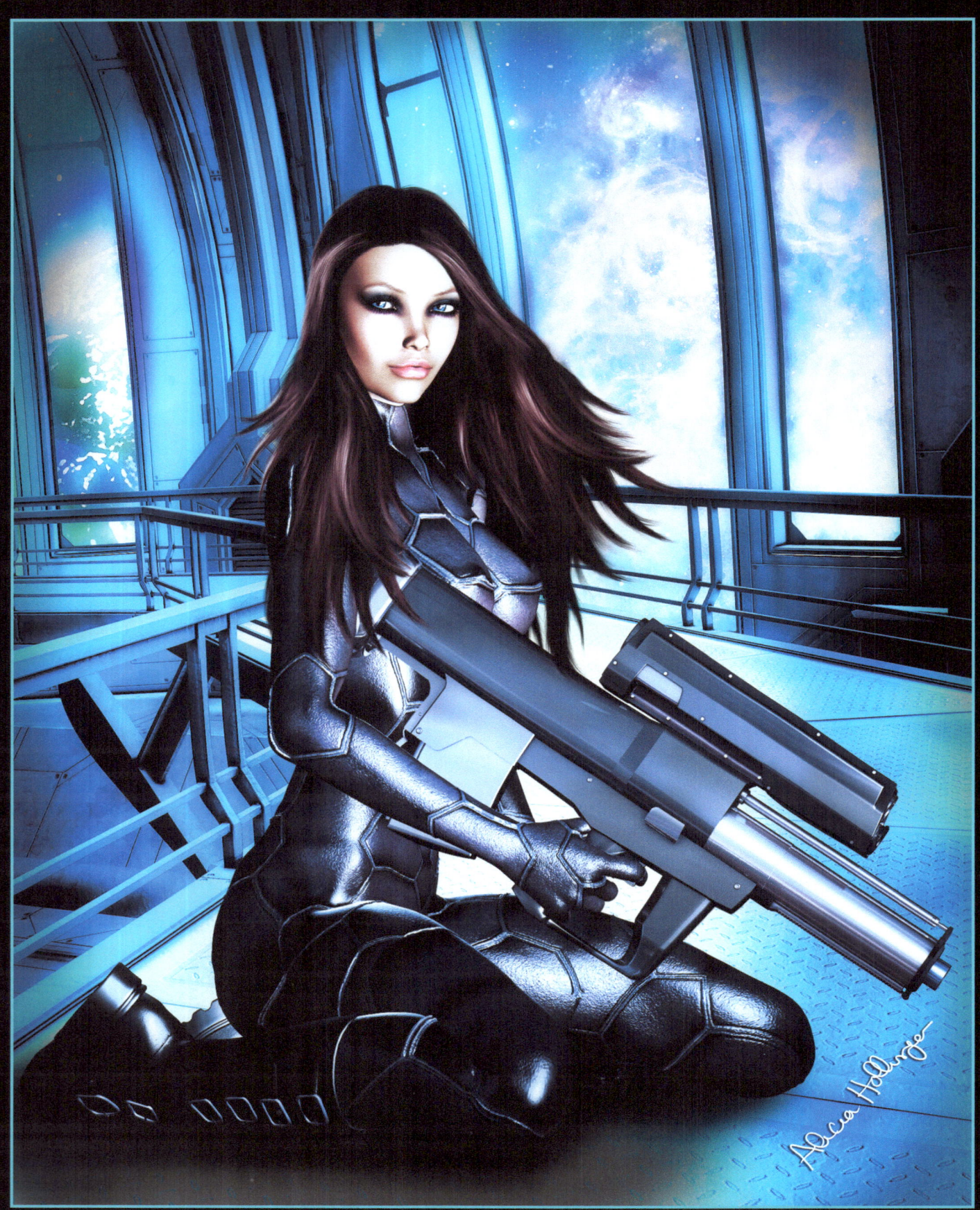

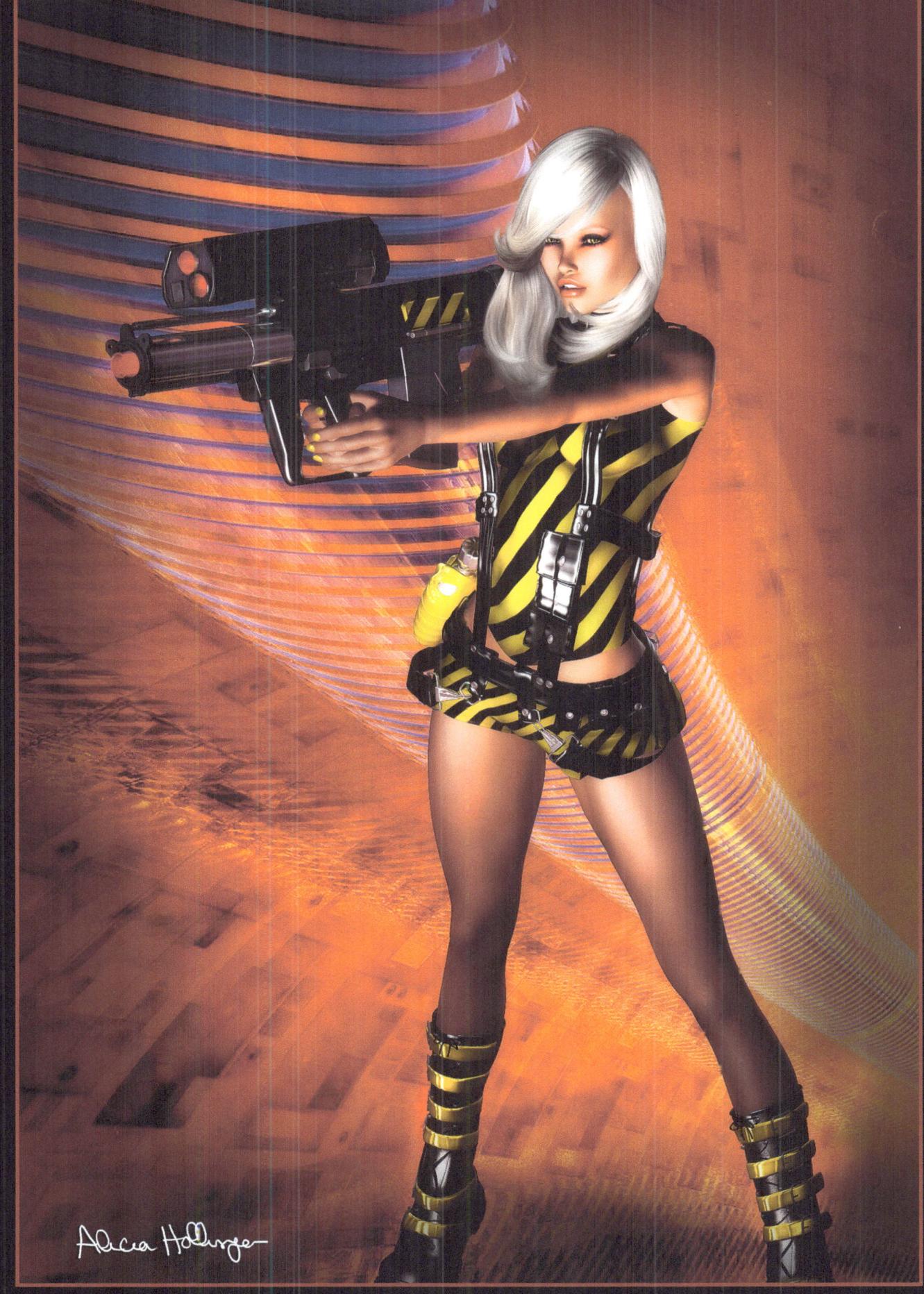

Alicia Hollinger

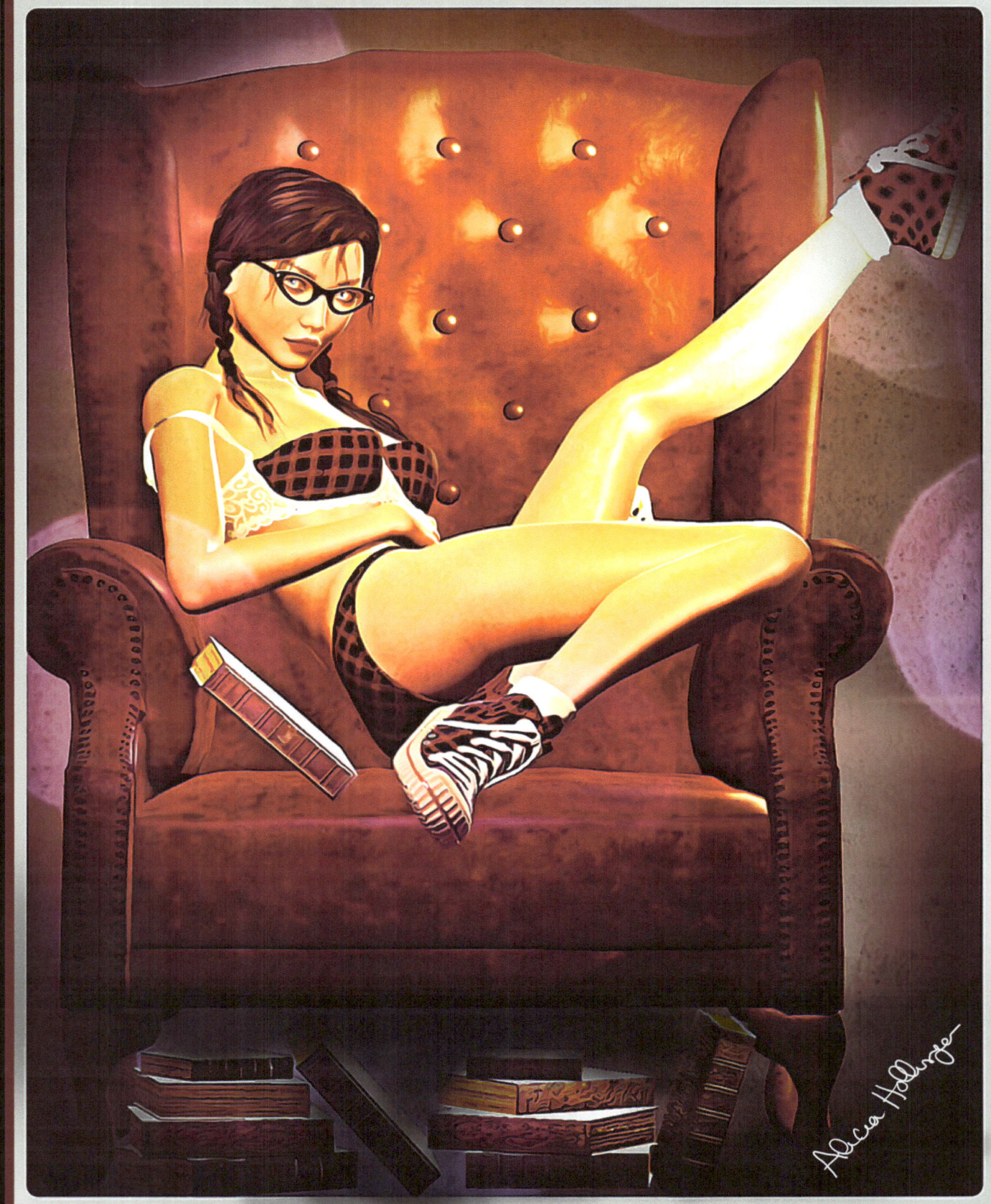

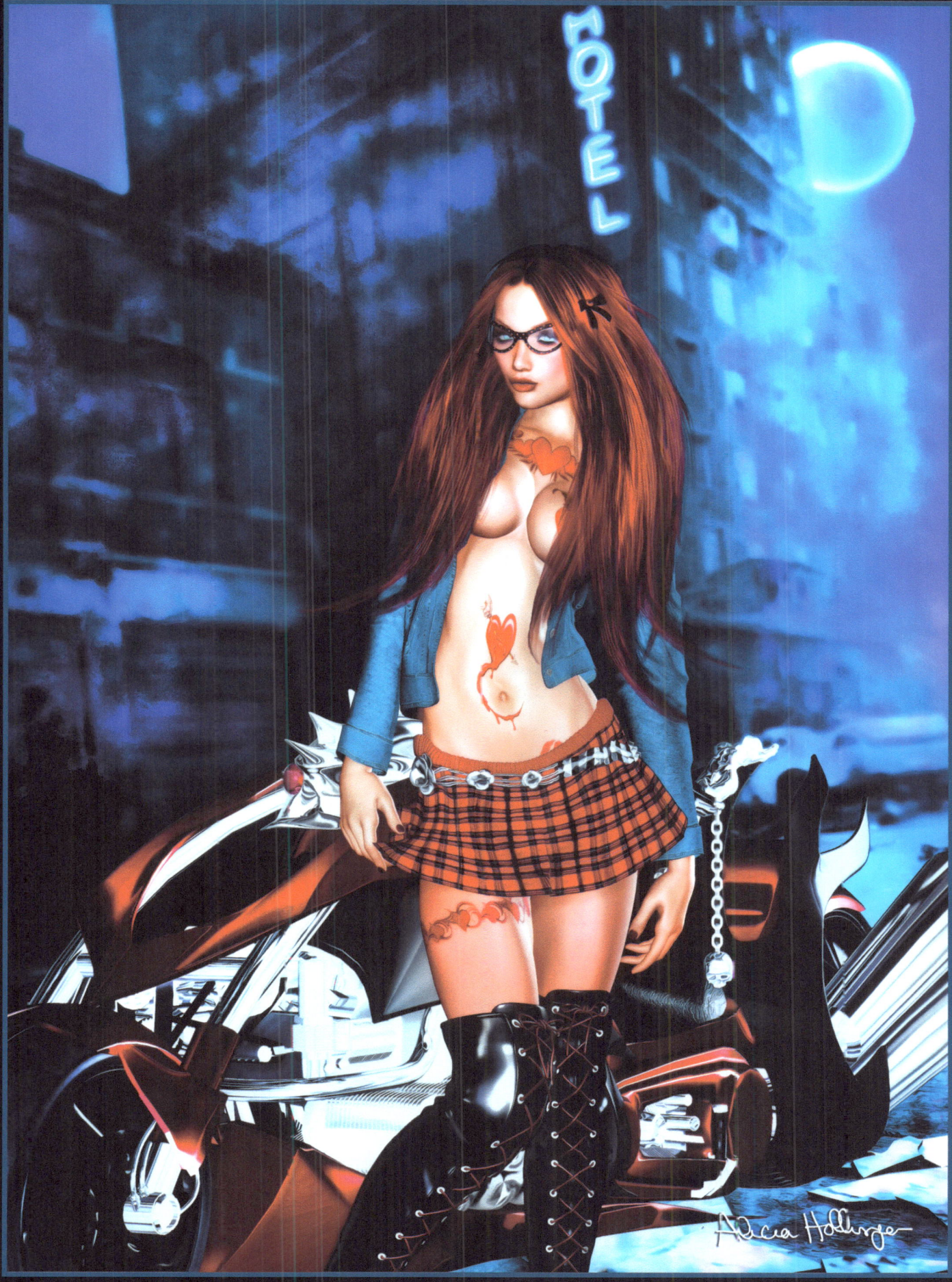

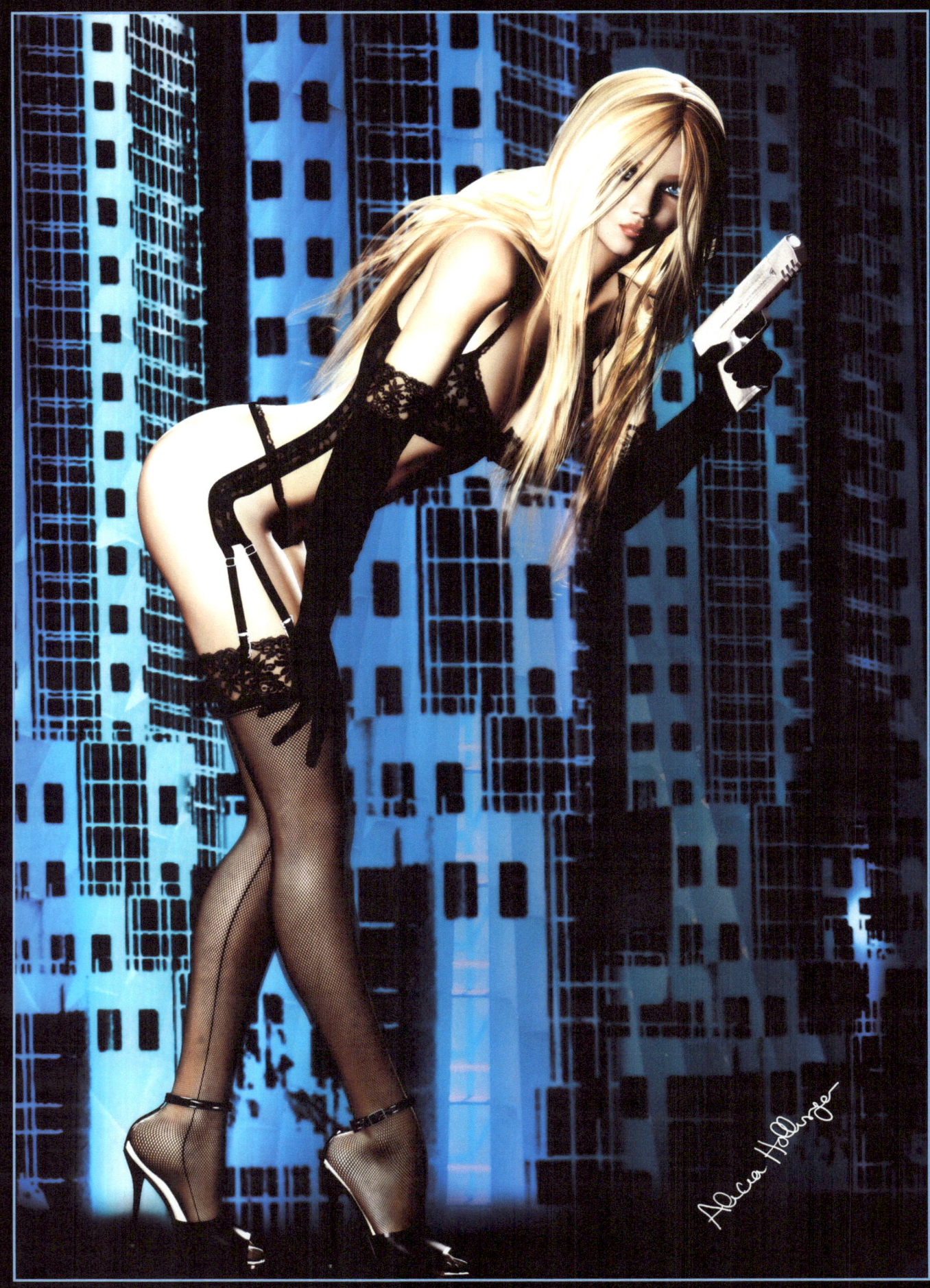

Alicia Hollinger

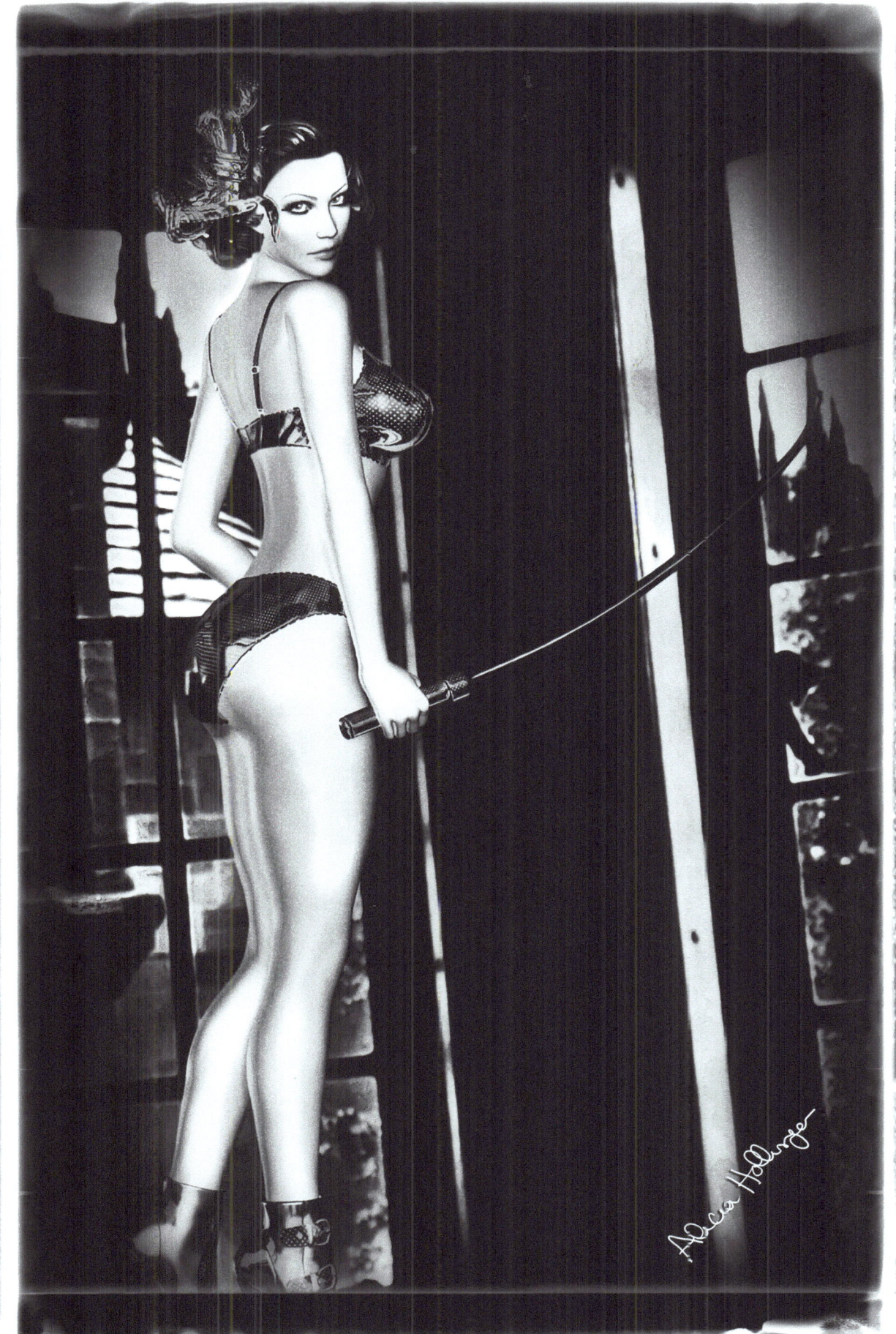

Alicia Hollinger

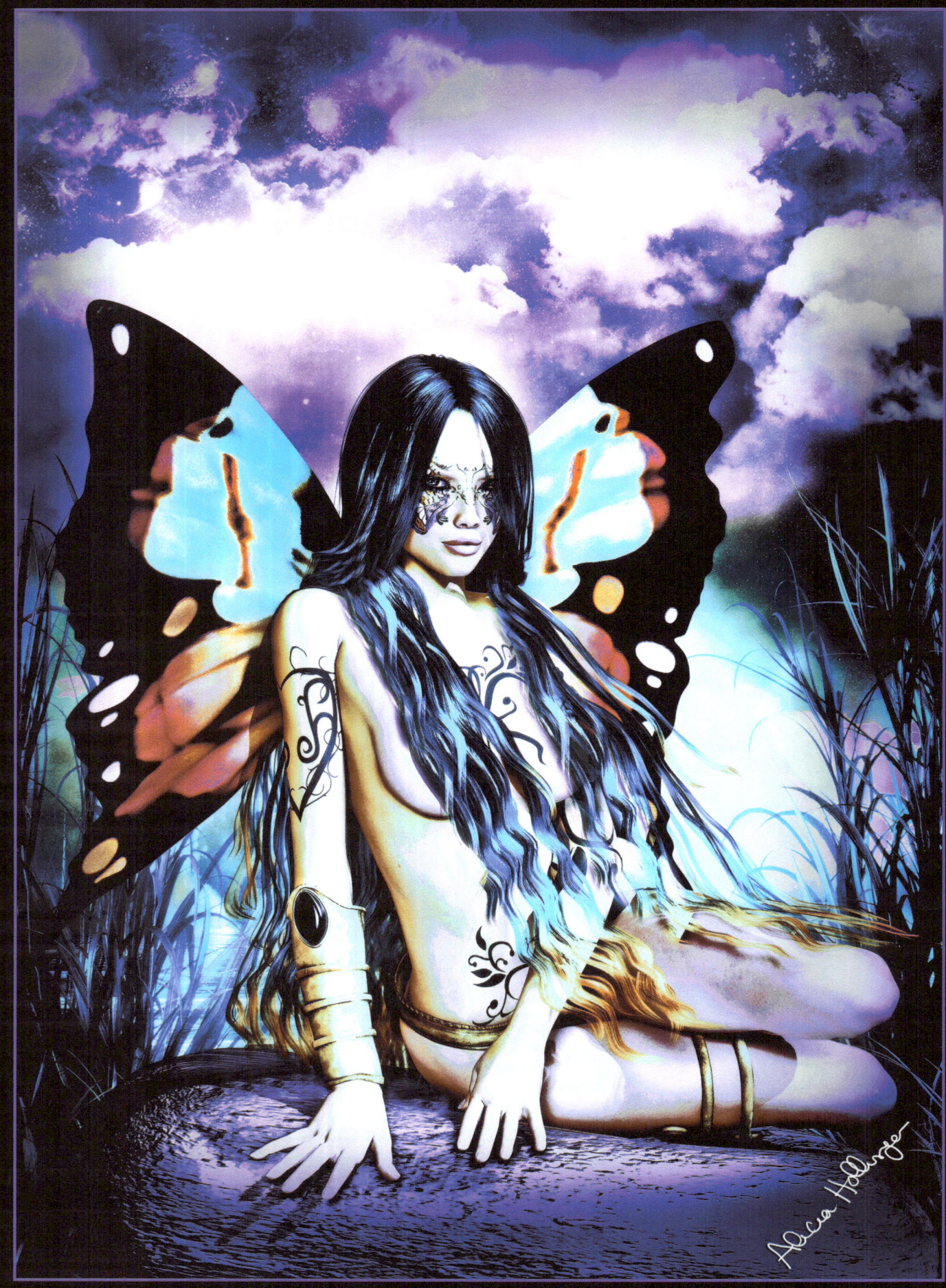

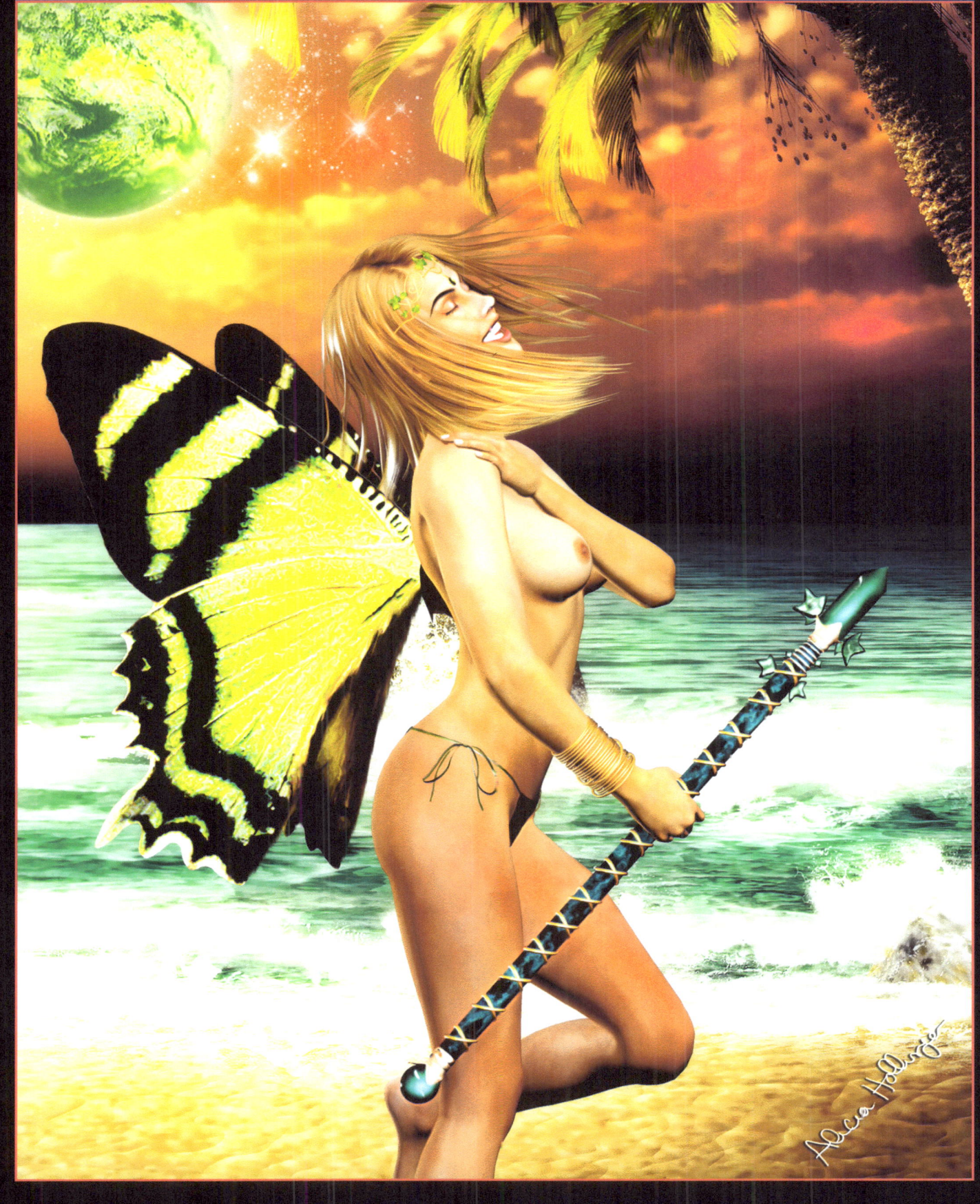

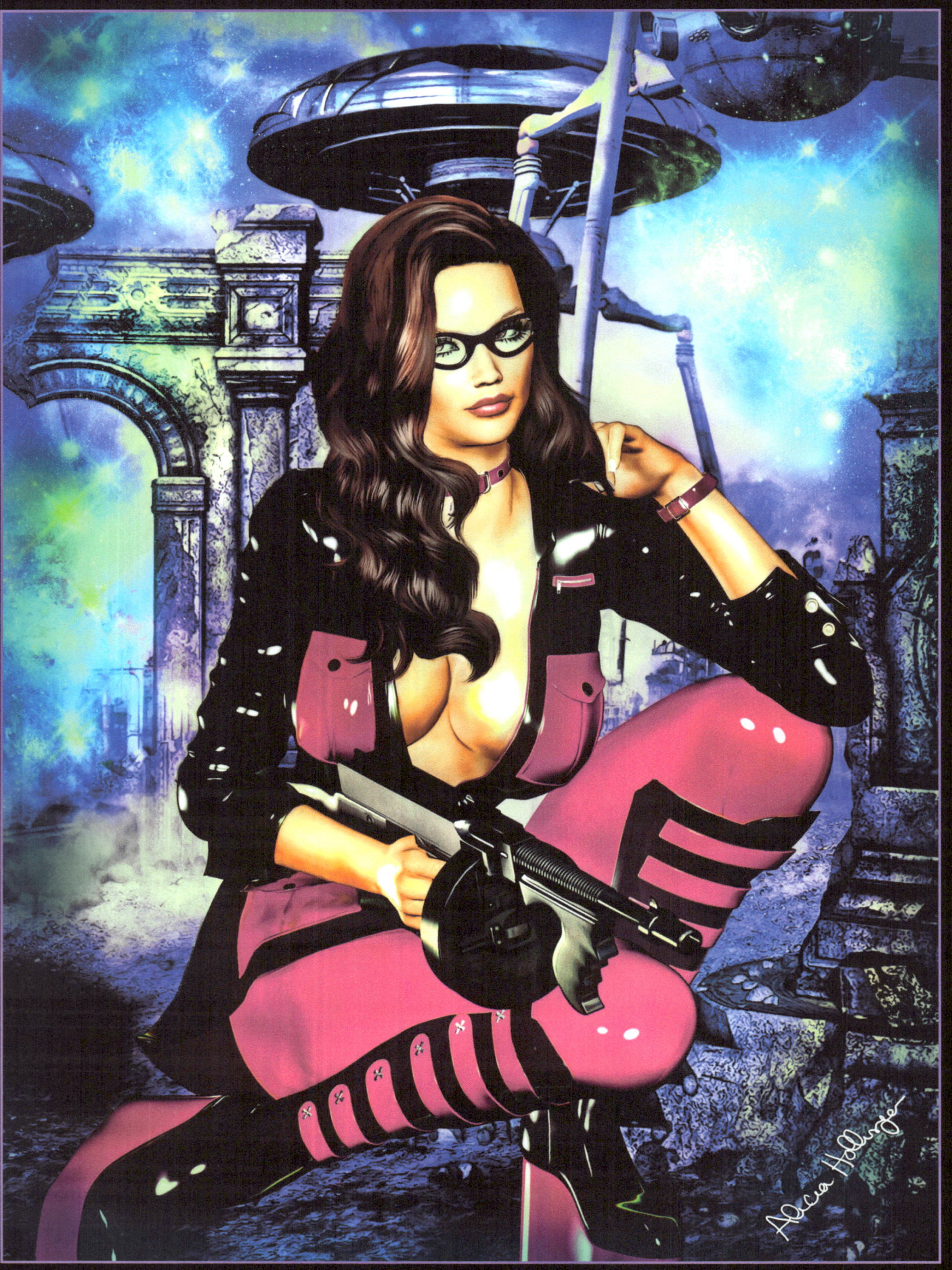

Alicia Hollinger

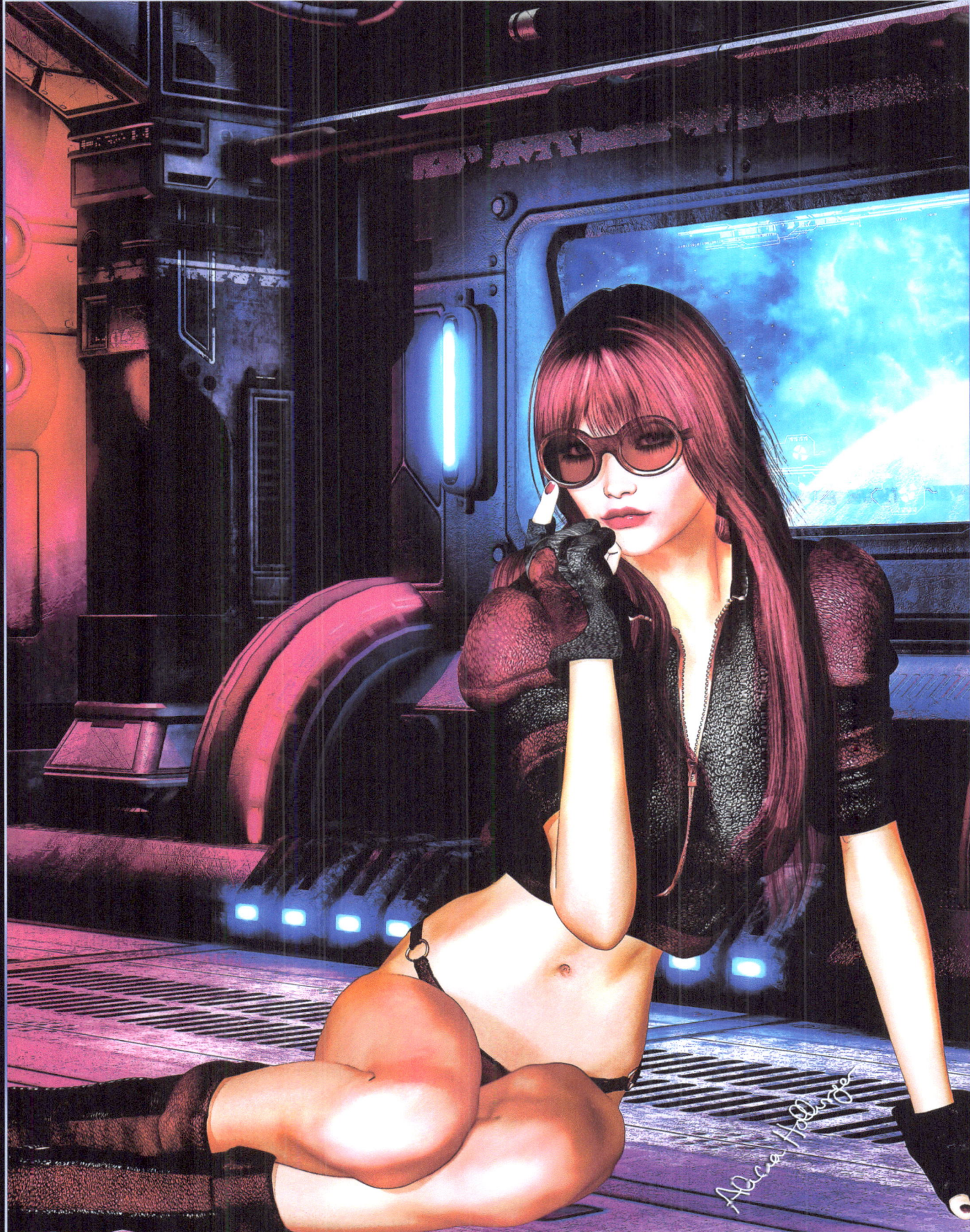

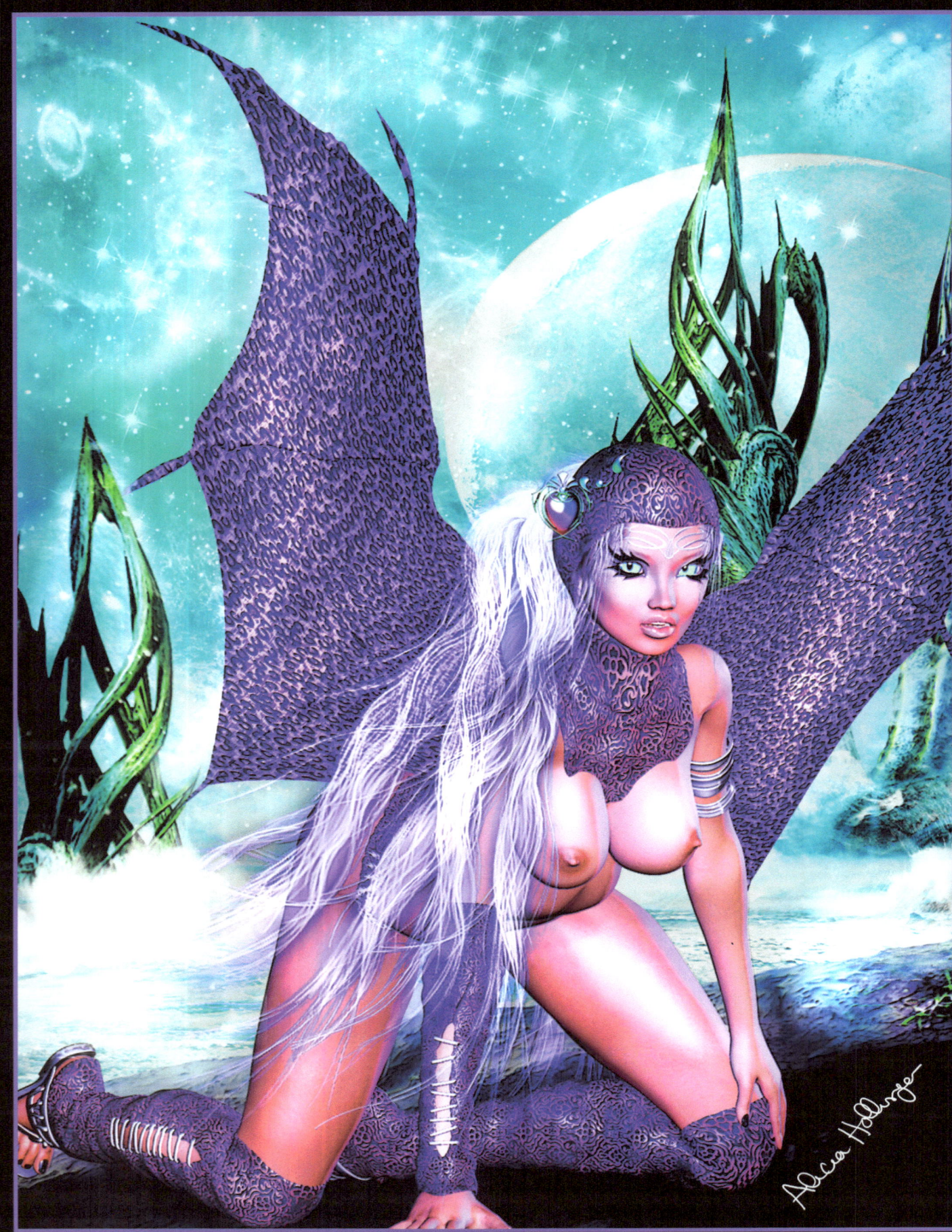

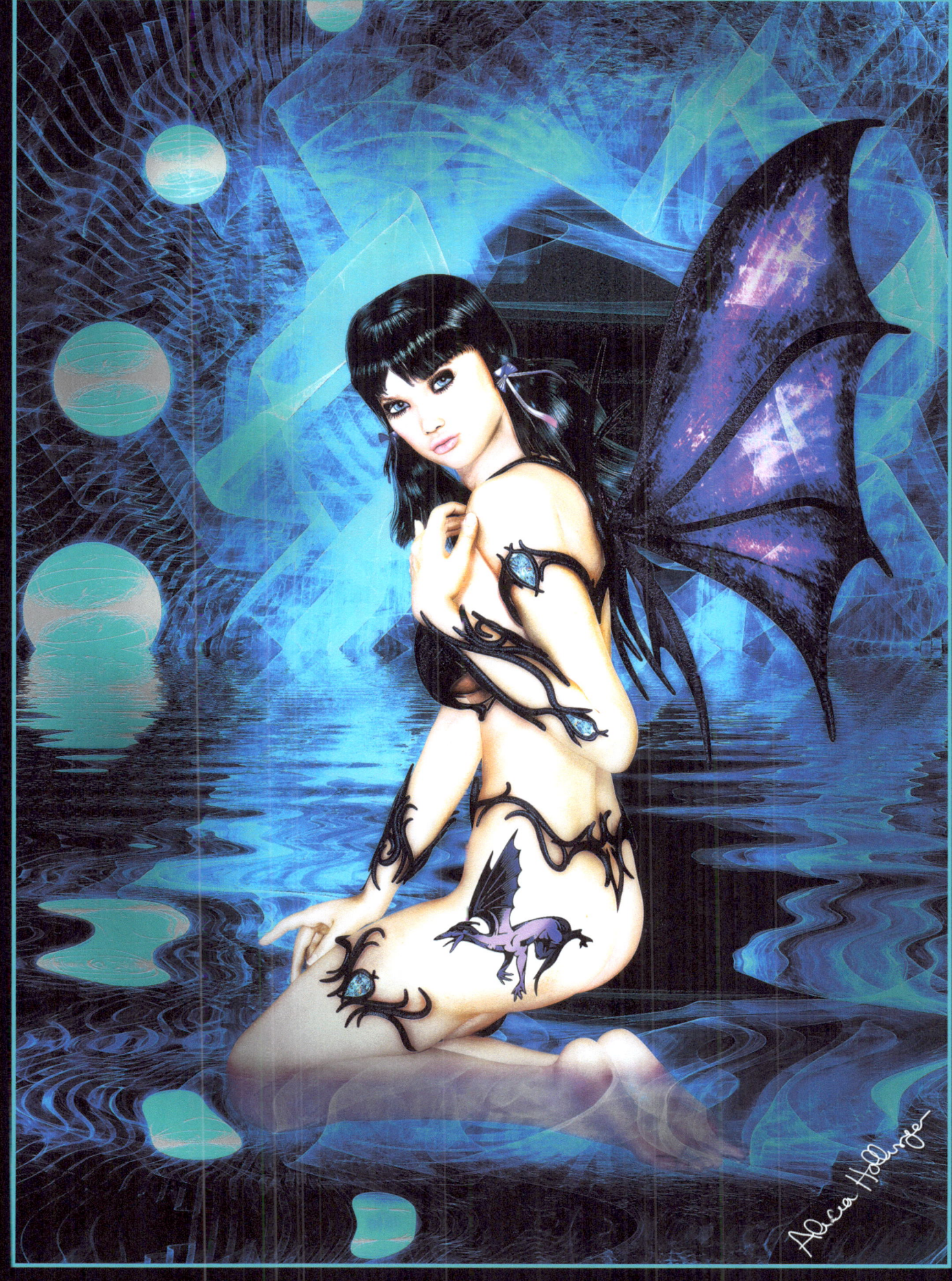

Alicia Hollinger

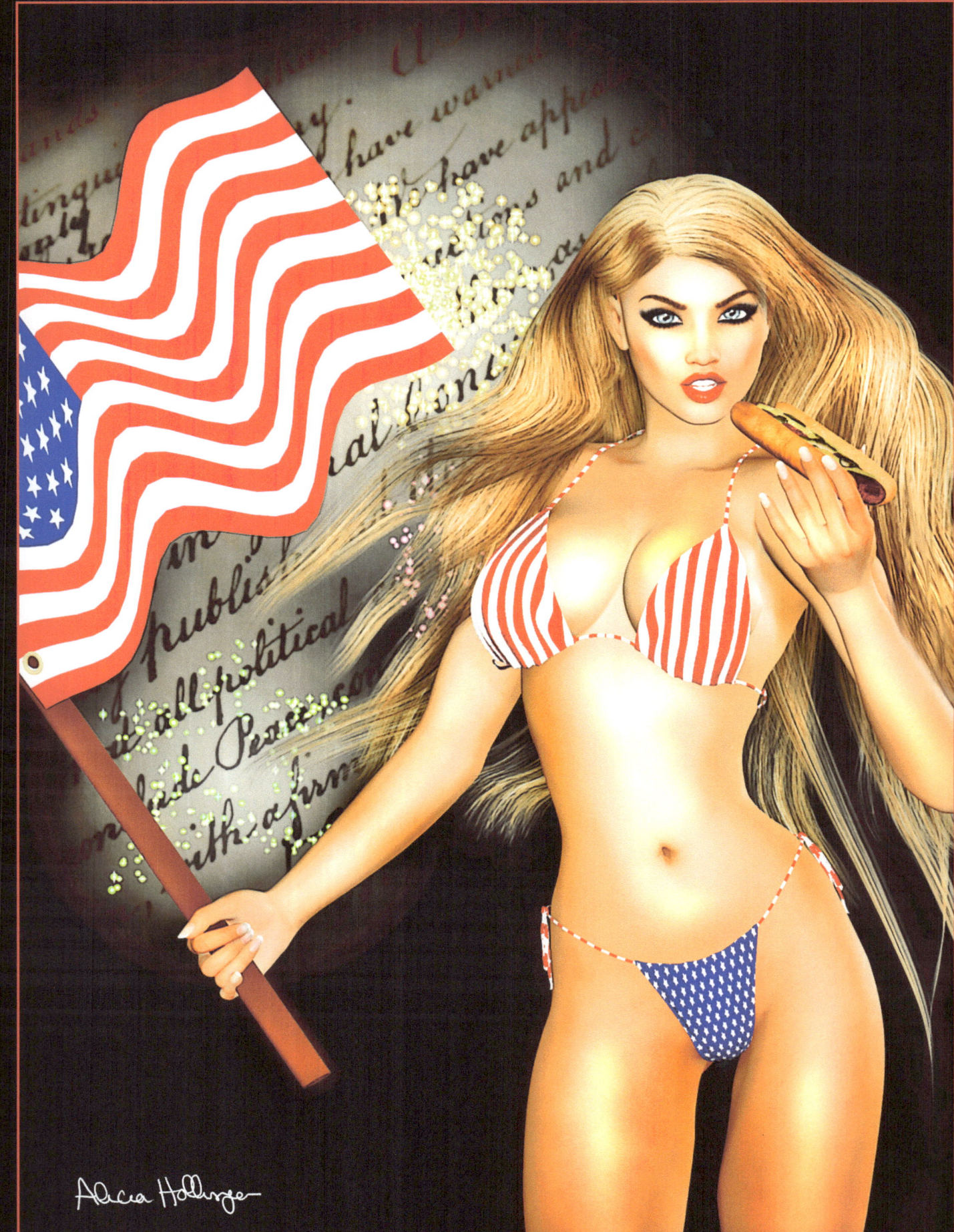

Alicia Hollinger

26

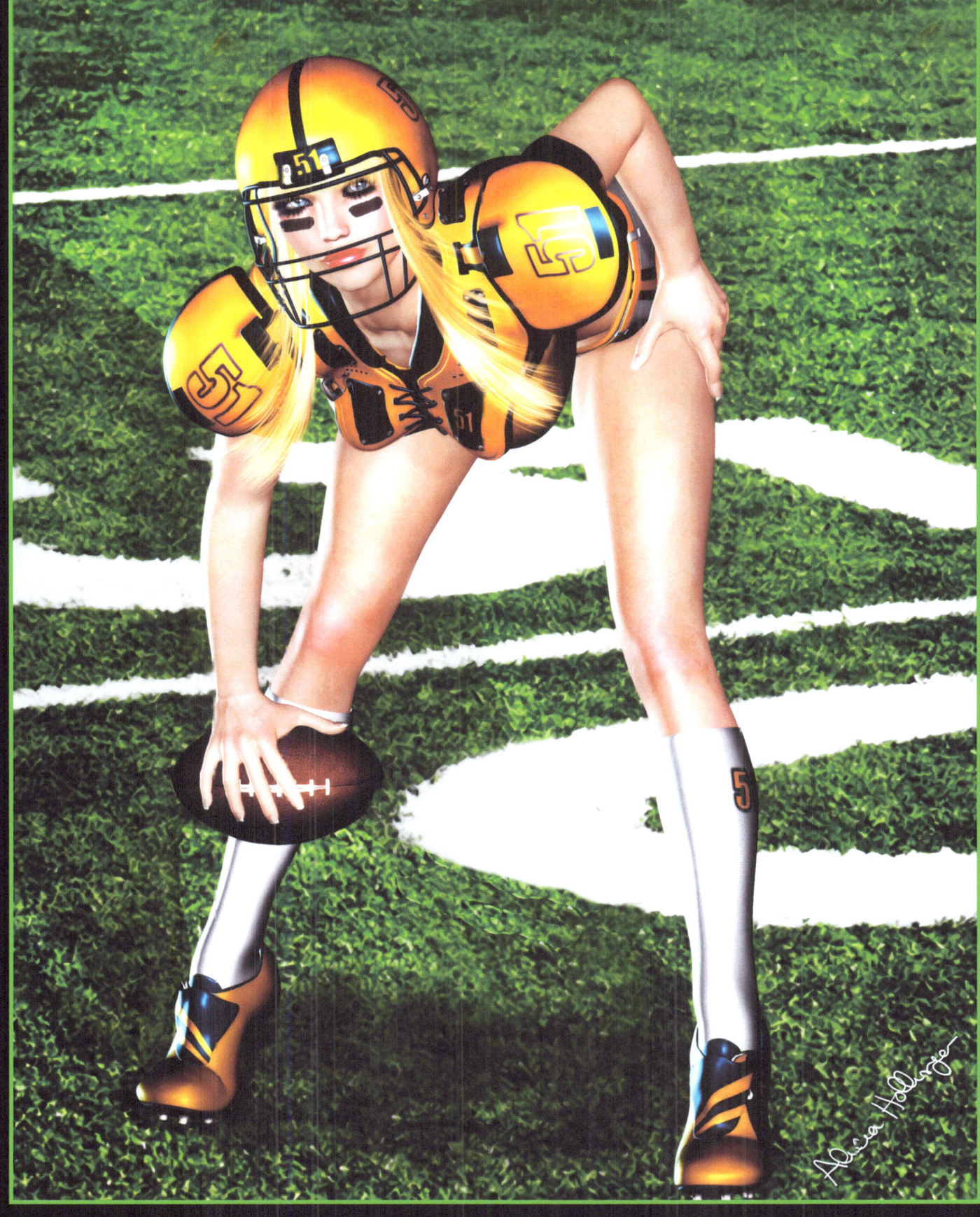

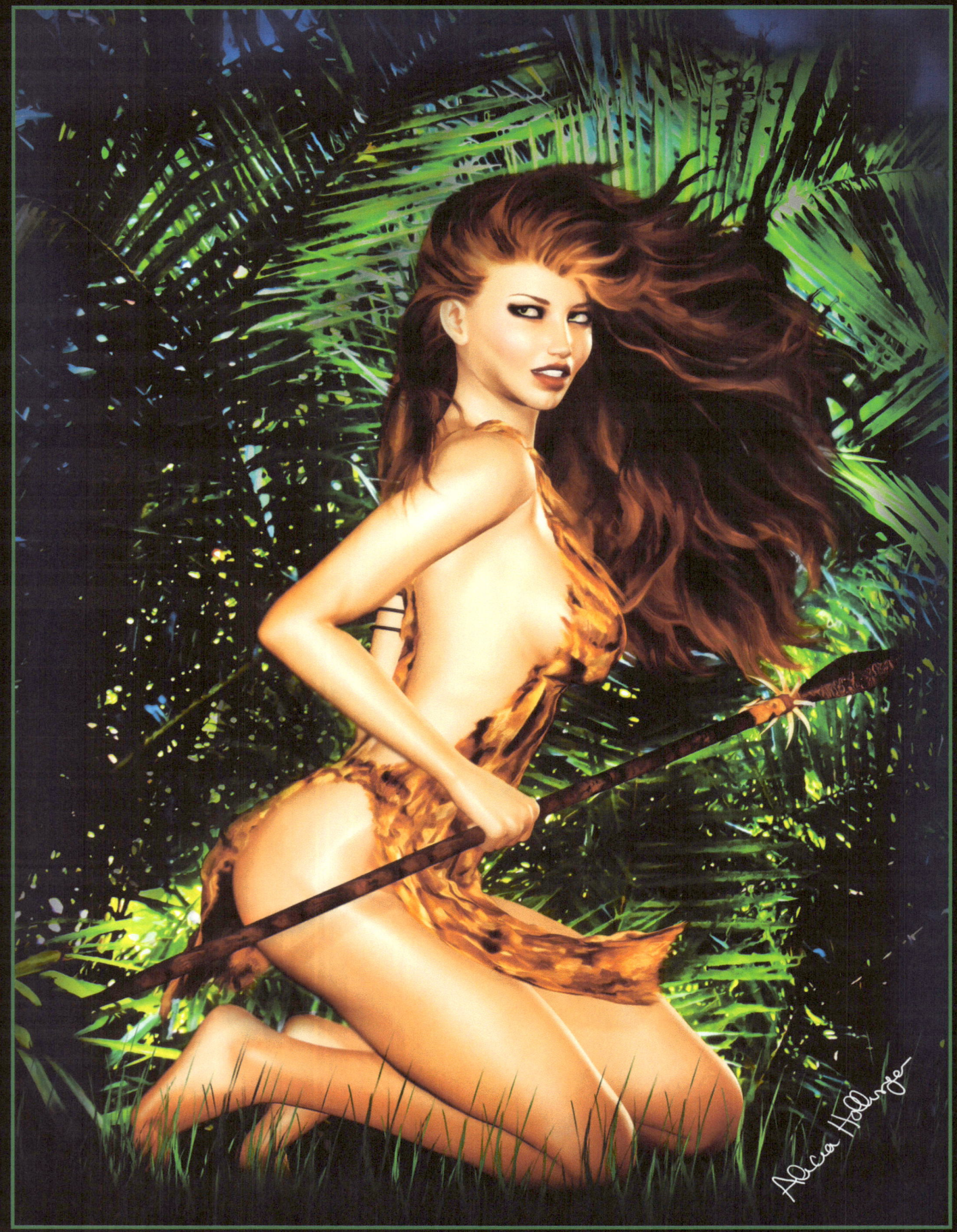

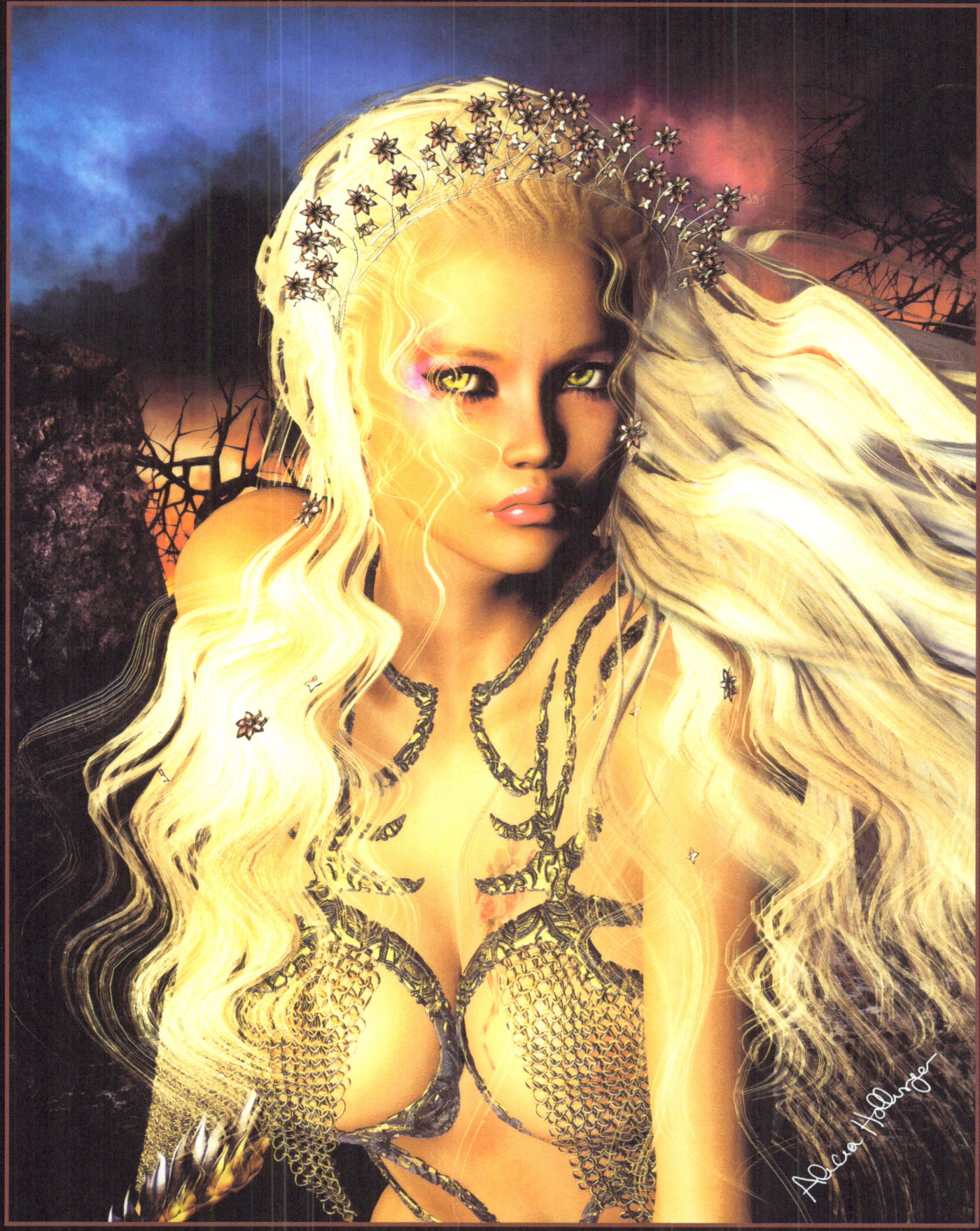

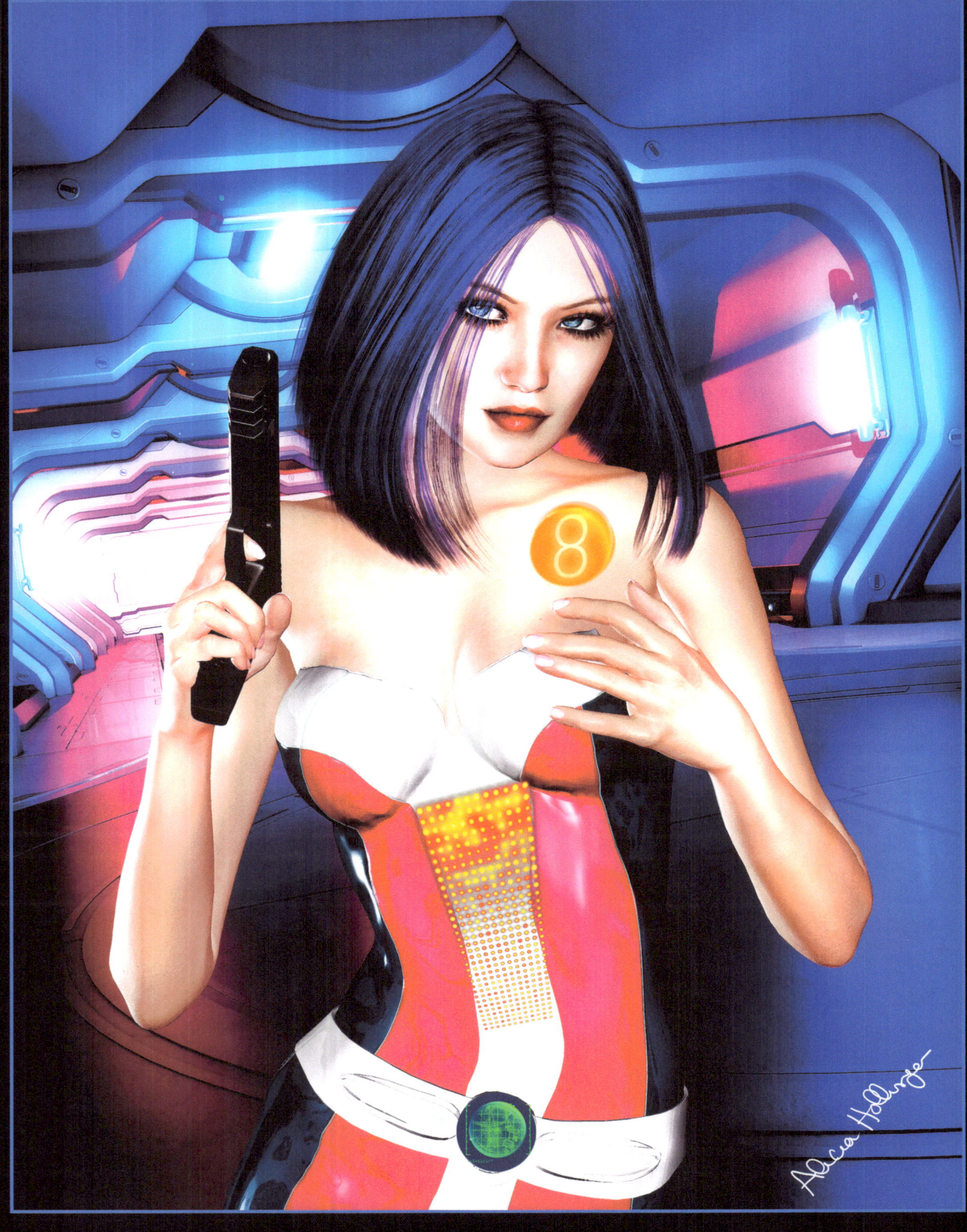

Alacia Hollinger

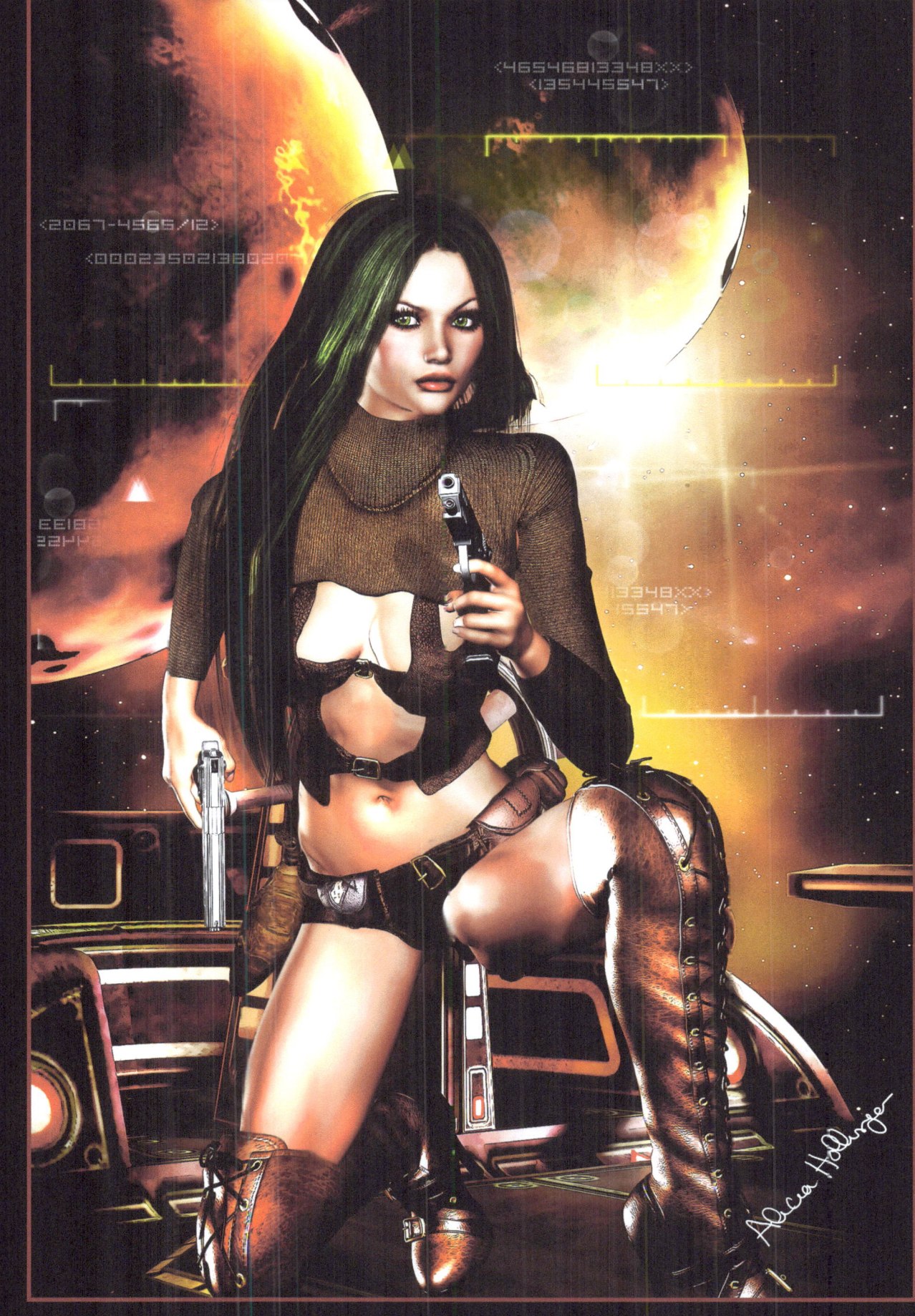

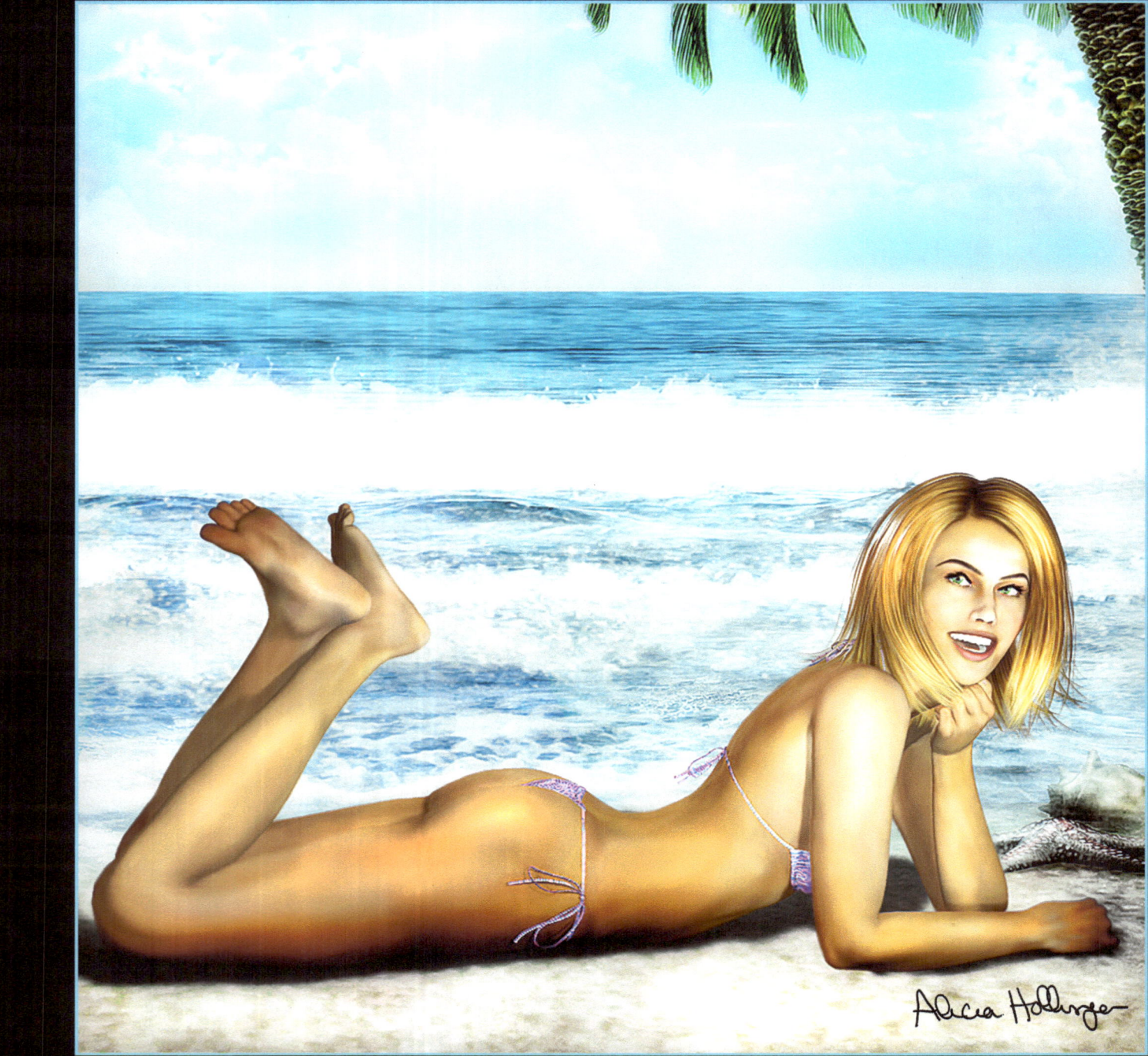

Alicia Hollinger

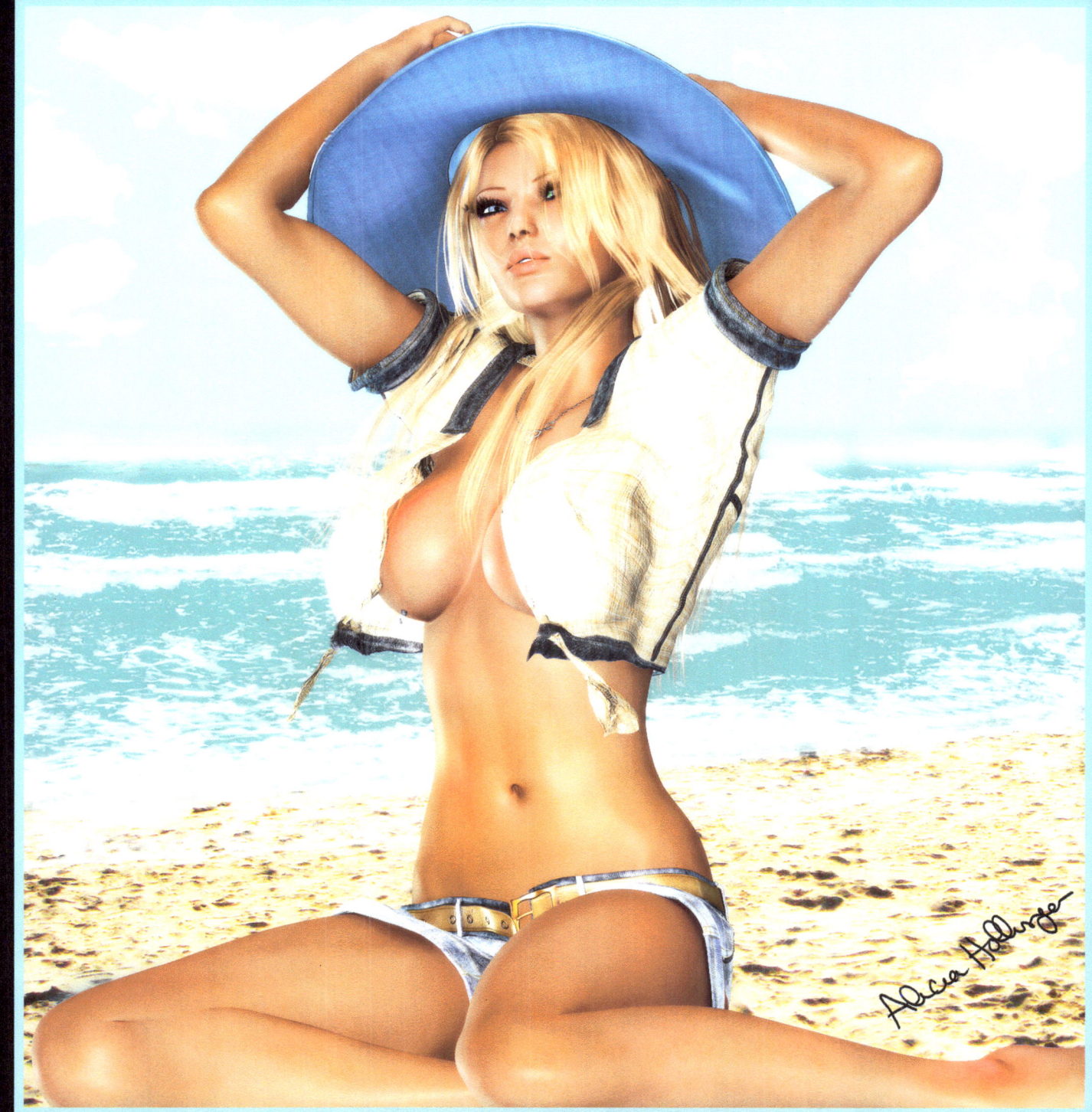

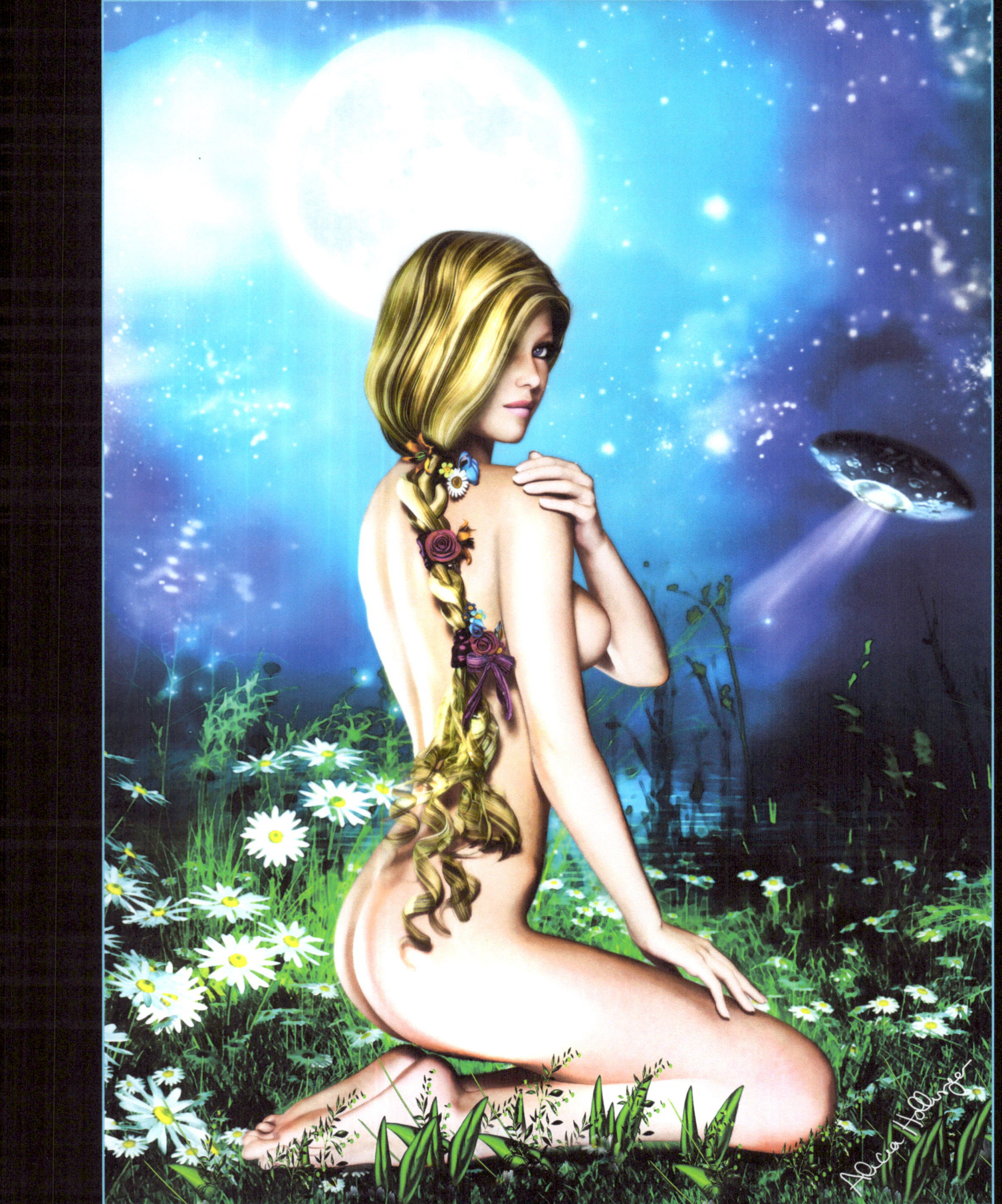

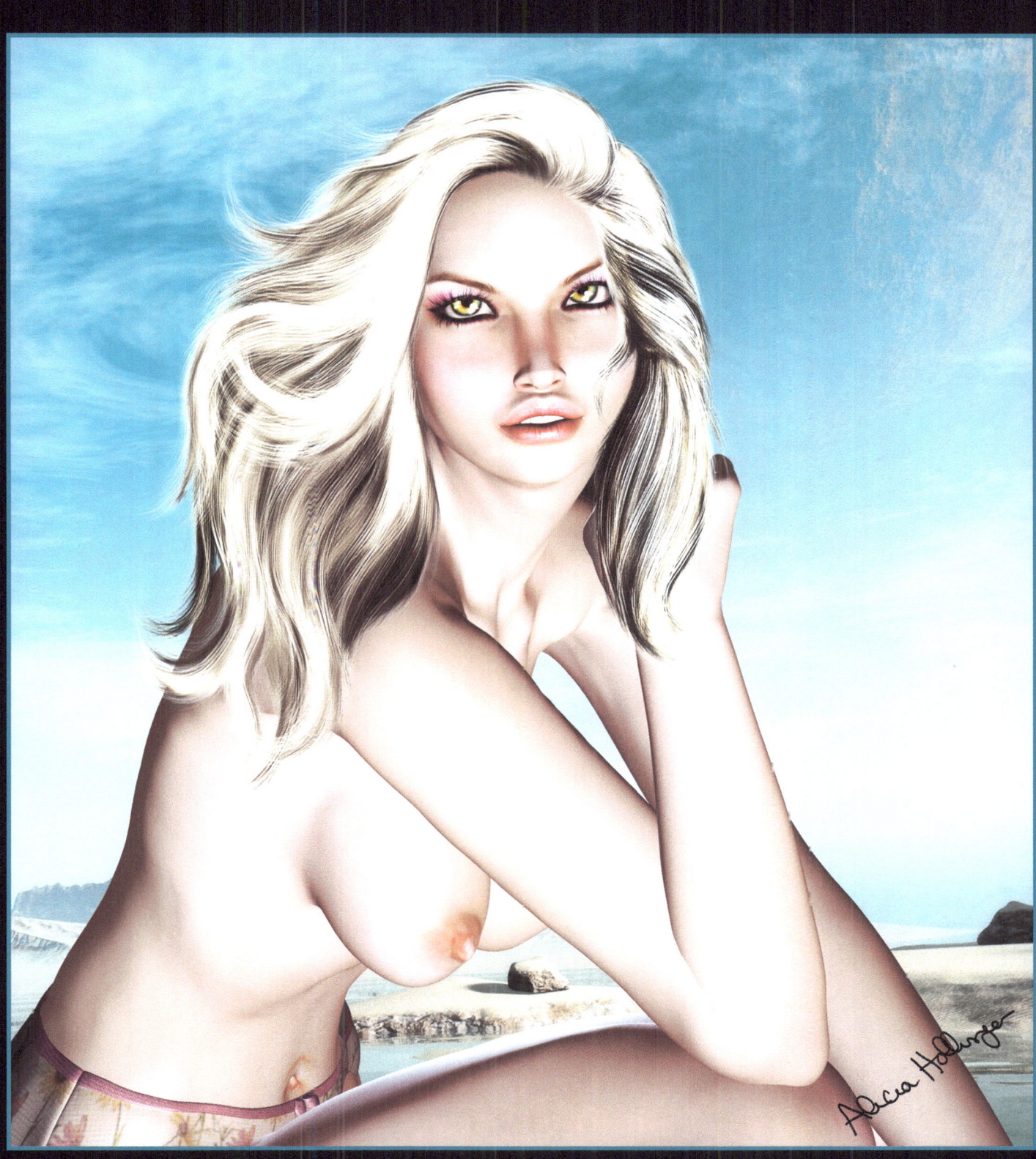

Alicia Hollinger

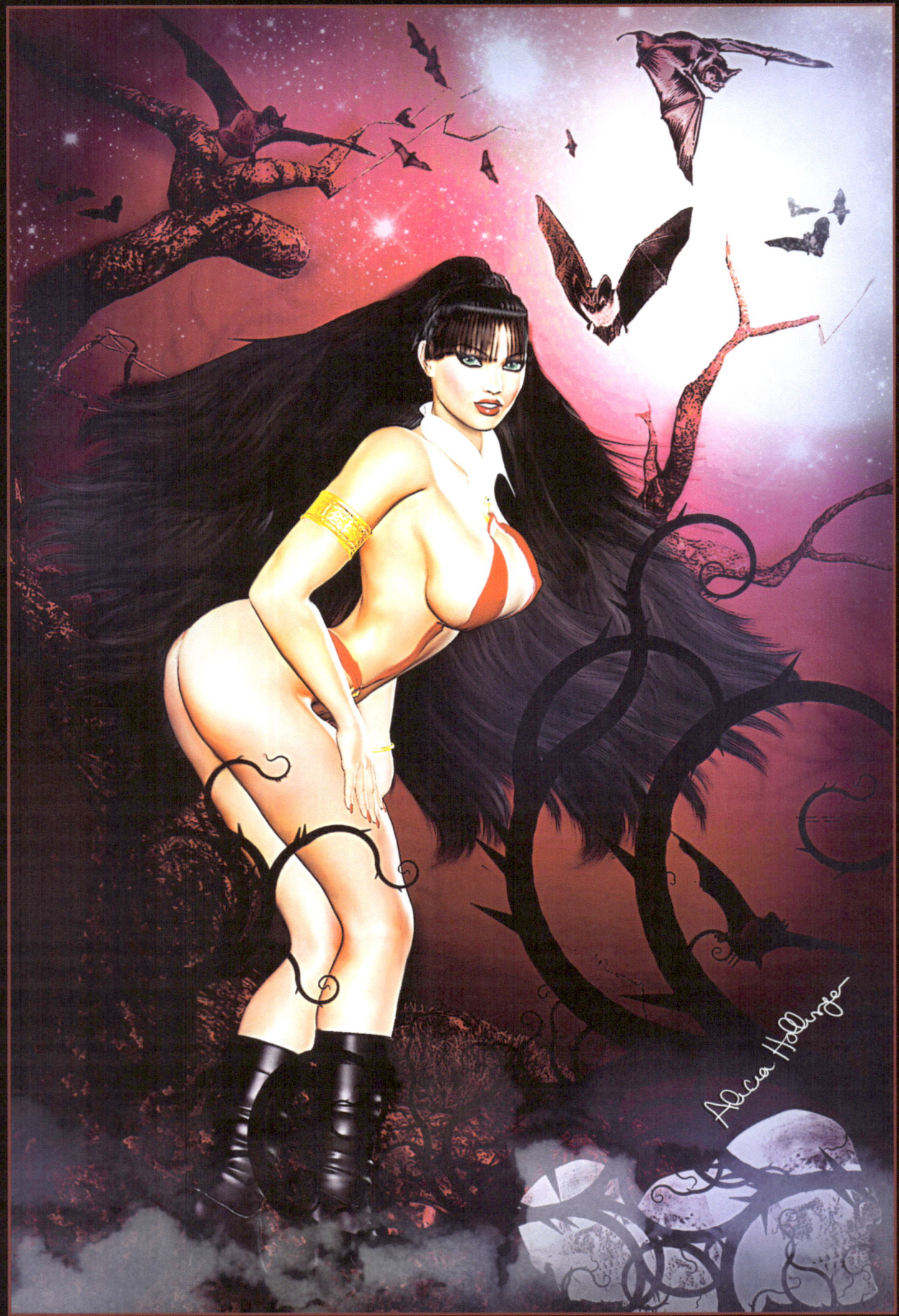

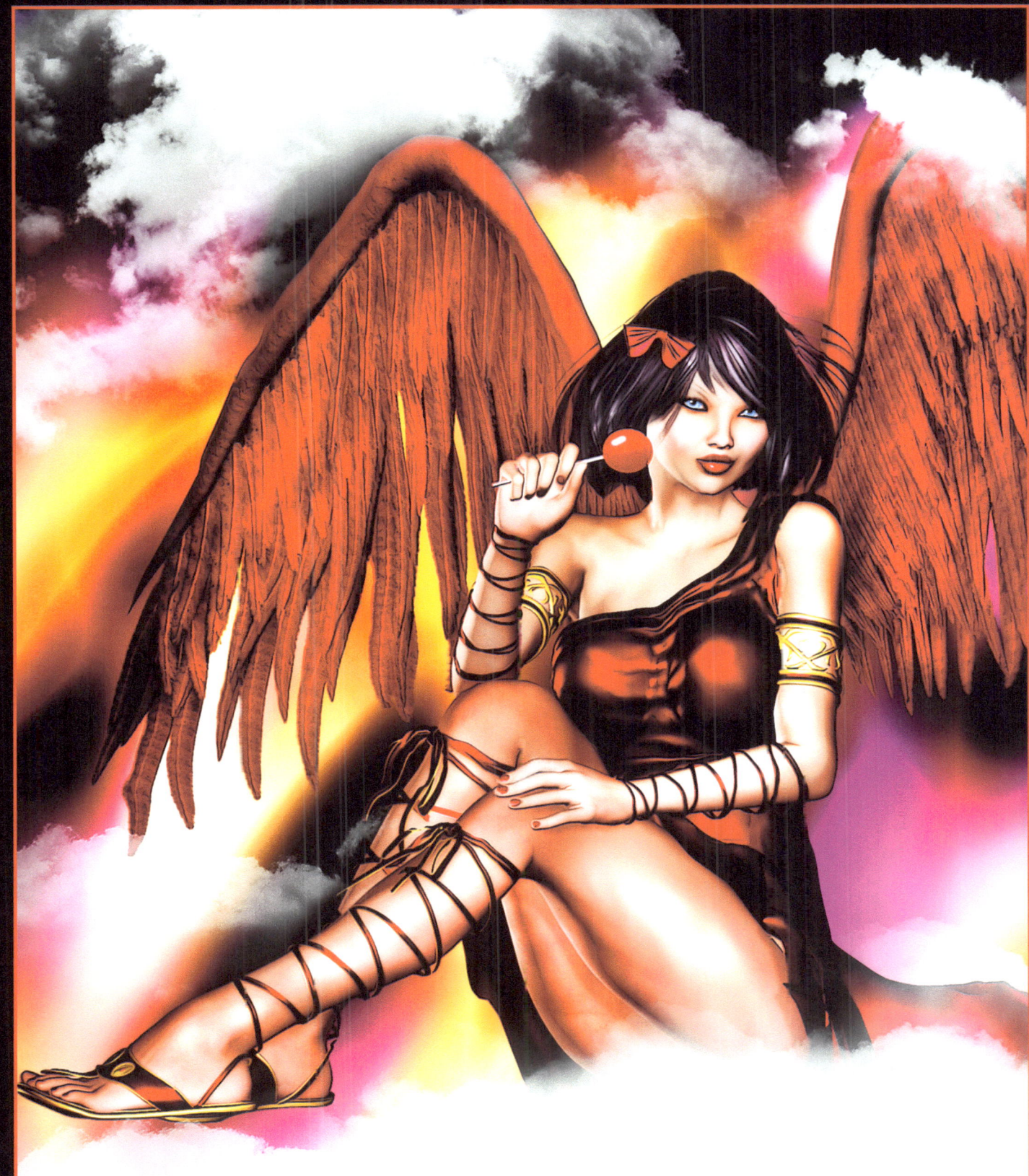

Alicia Hollinger

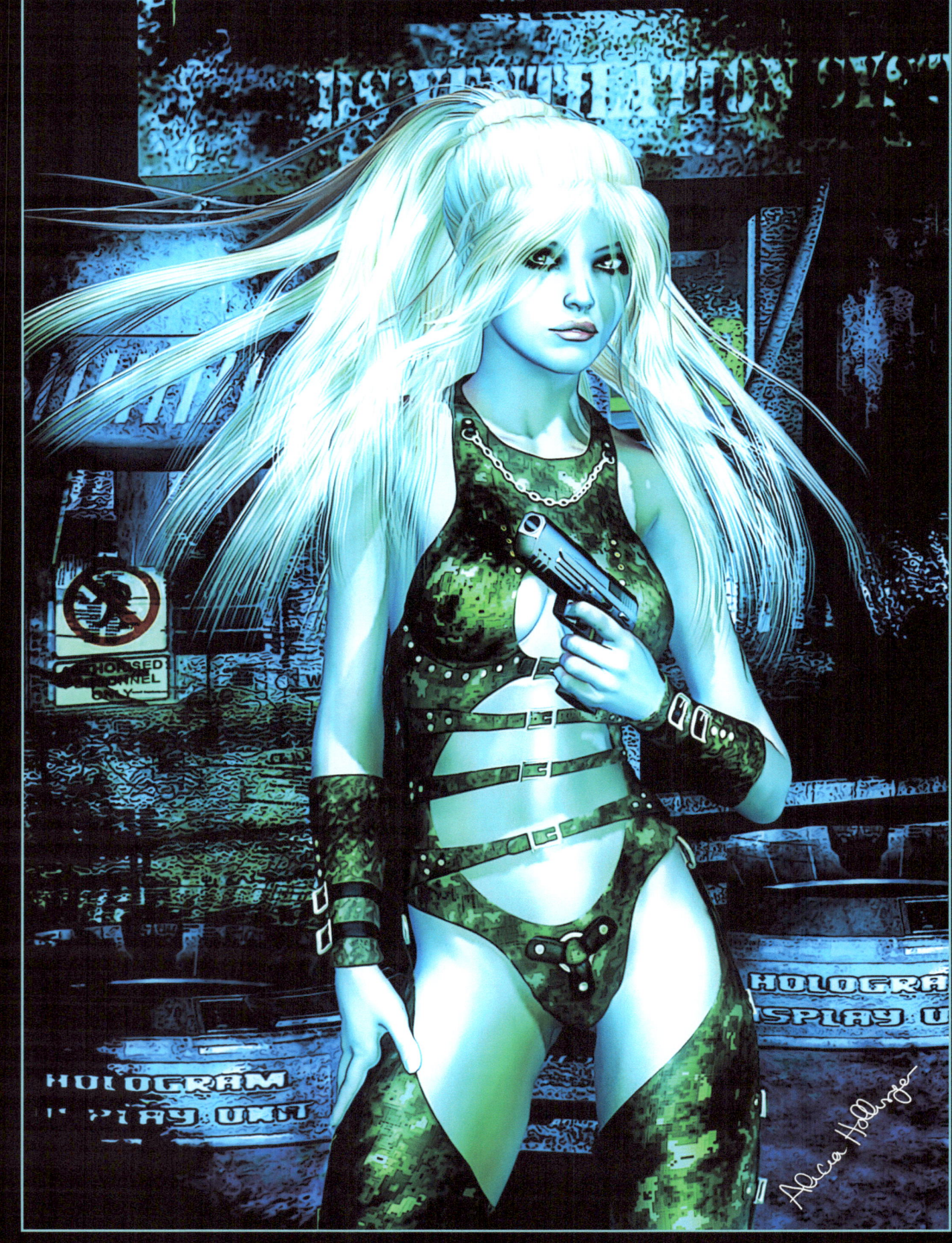

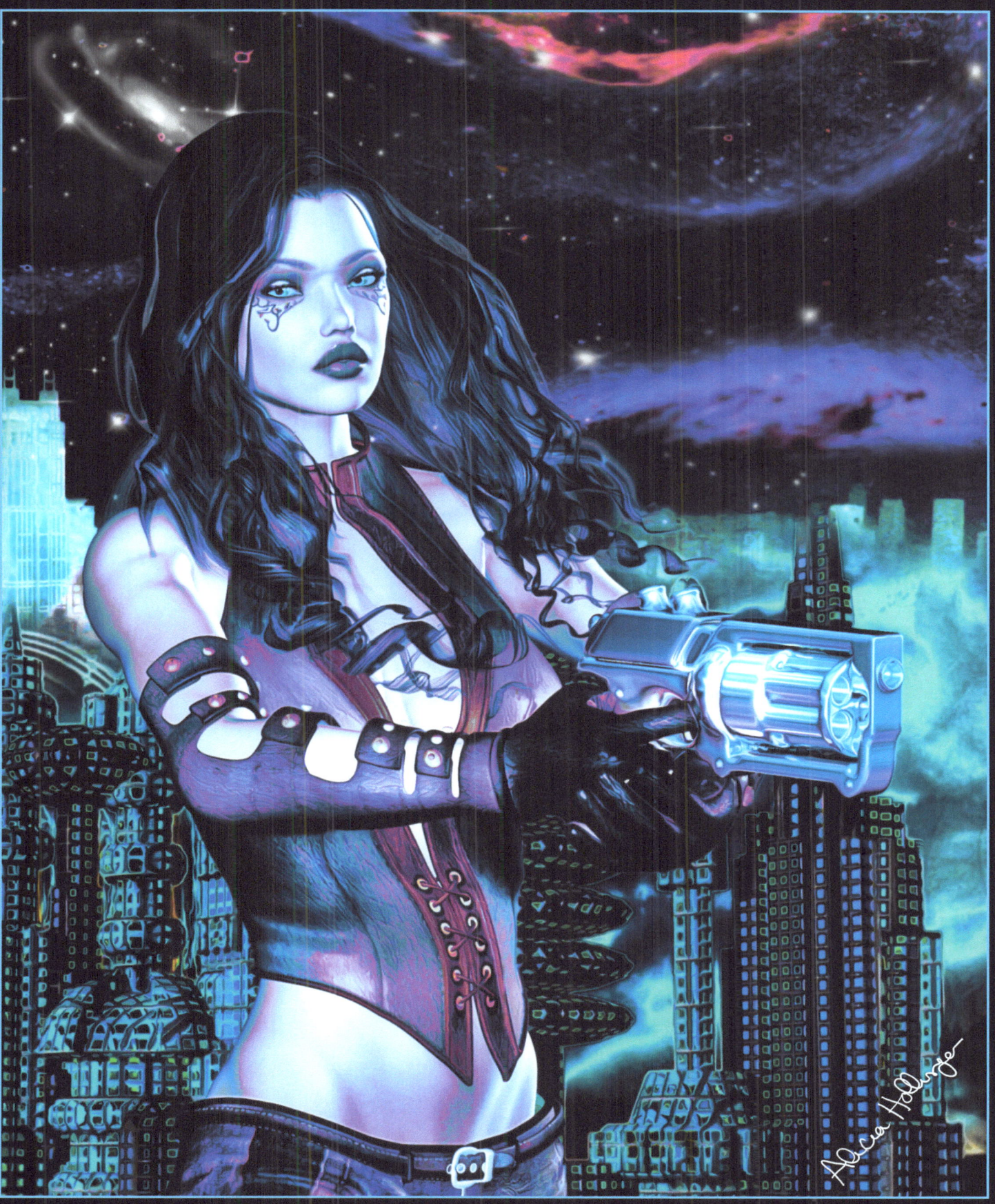

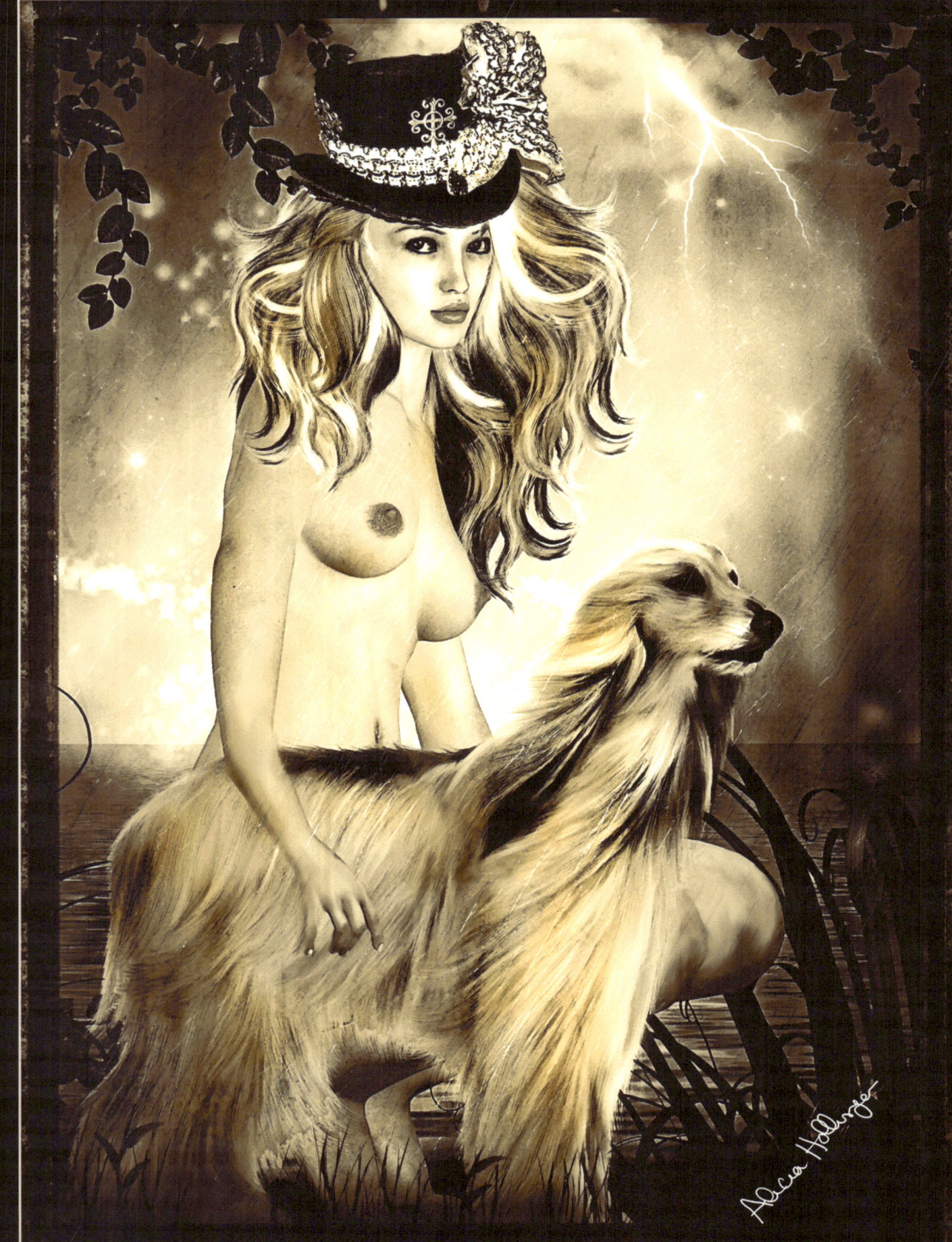

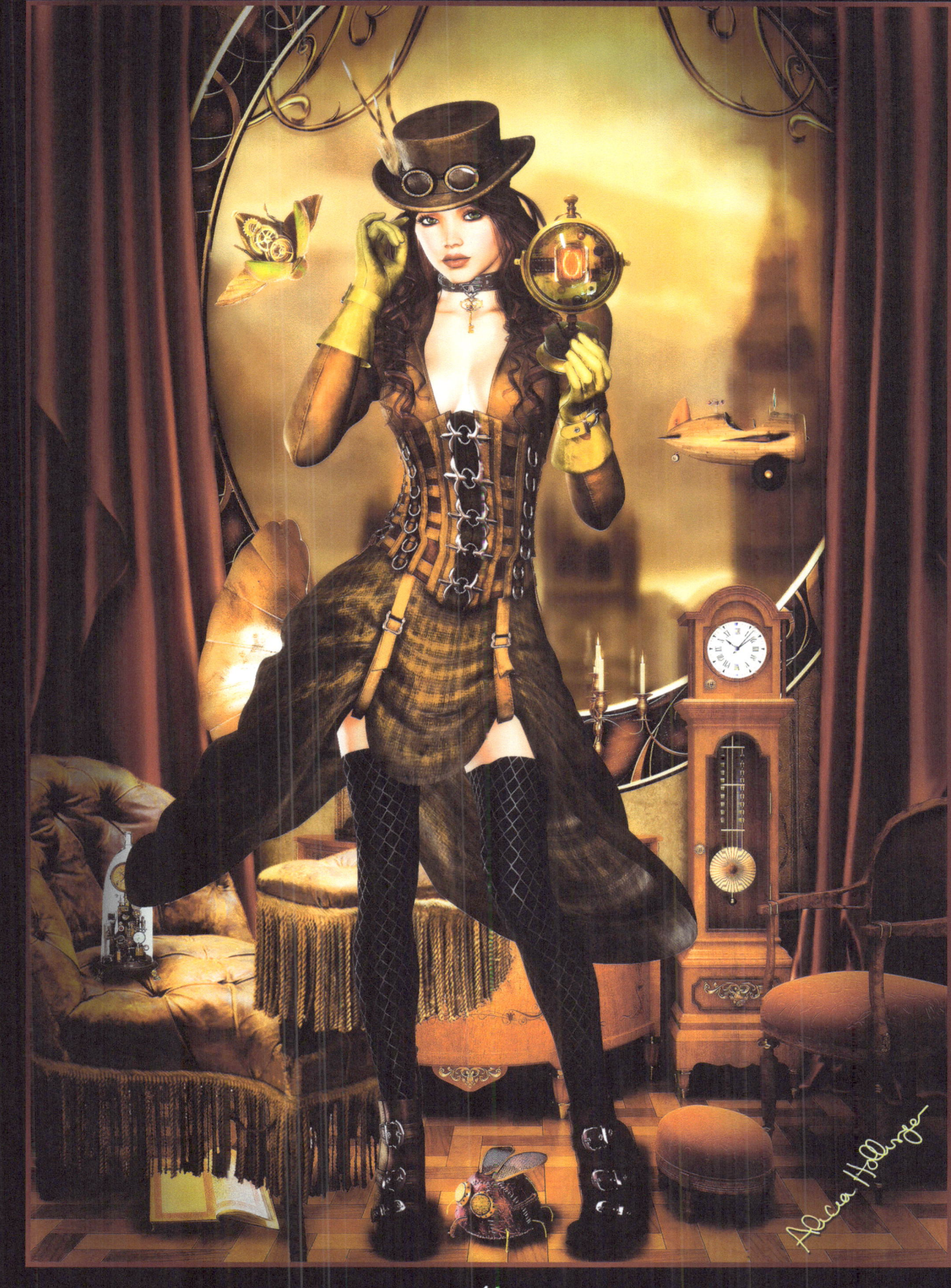

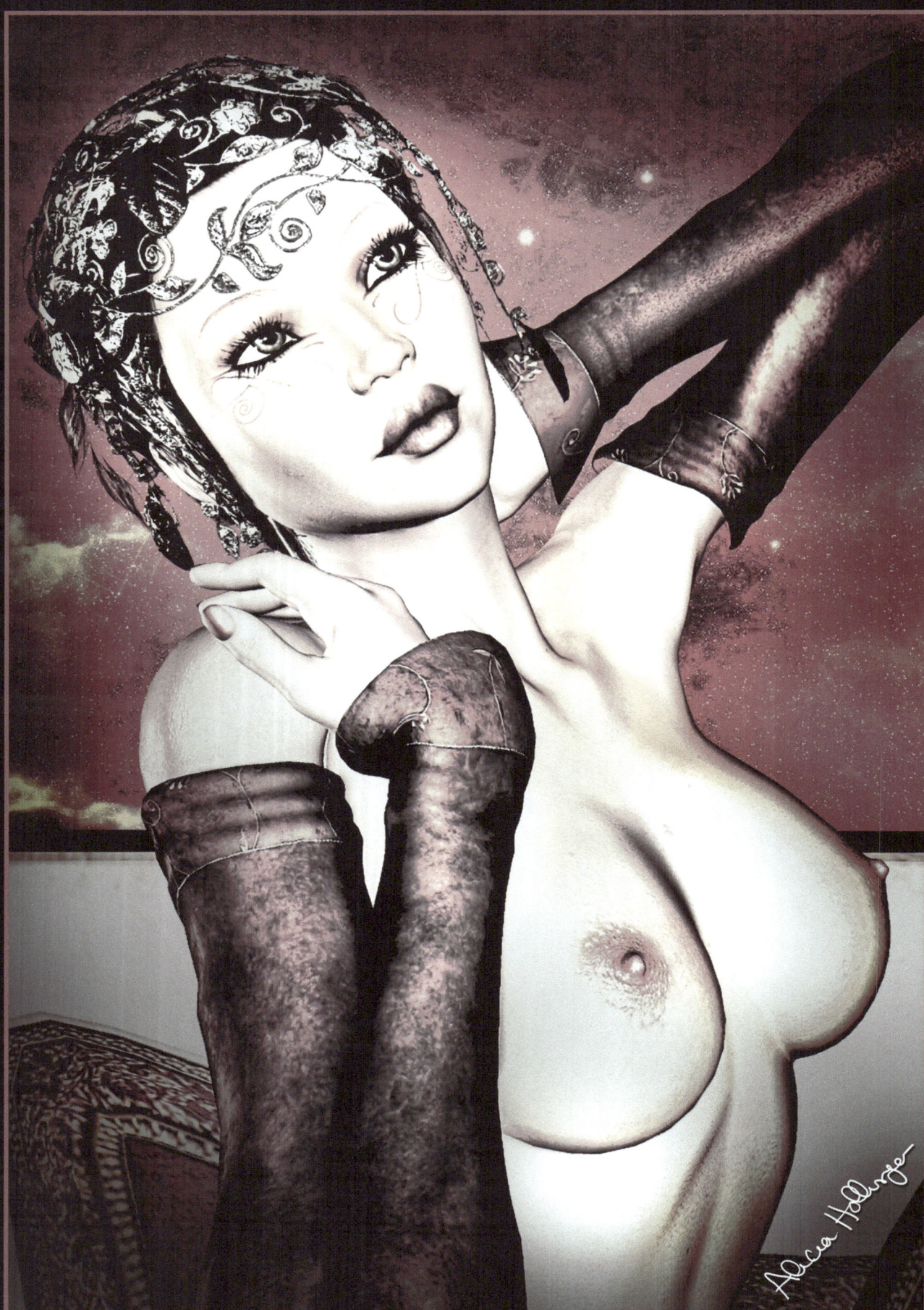

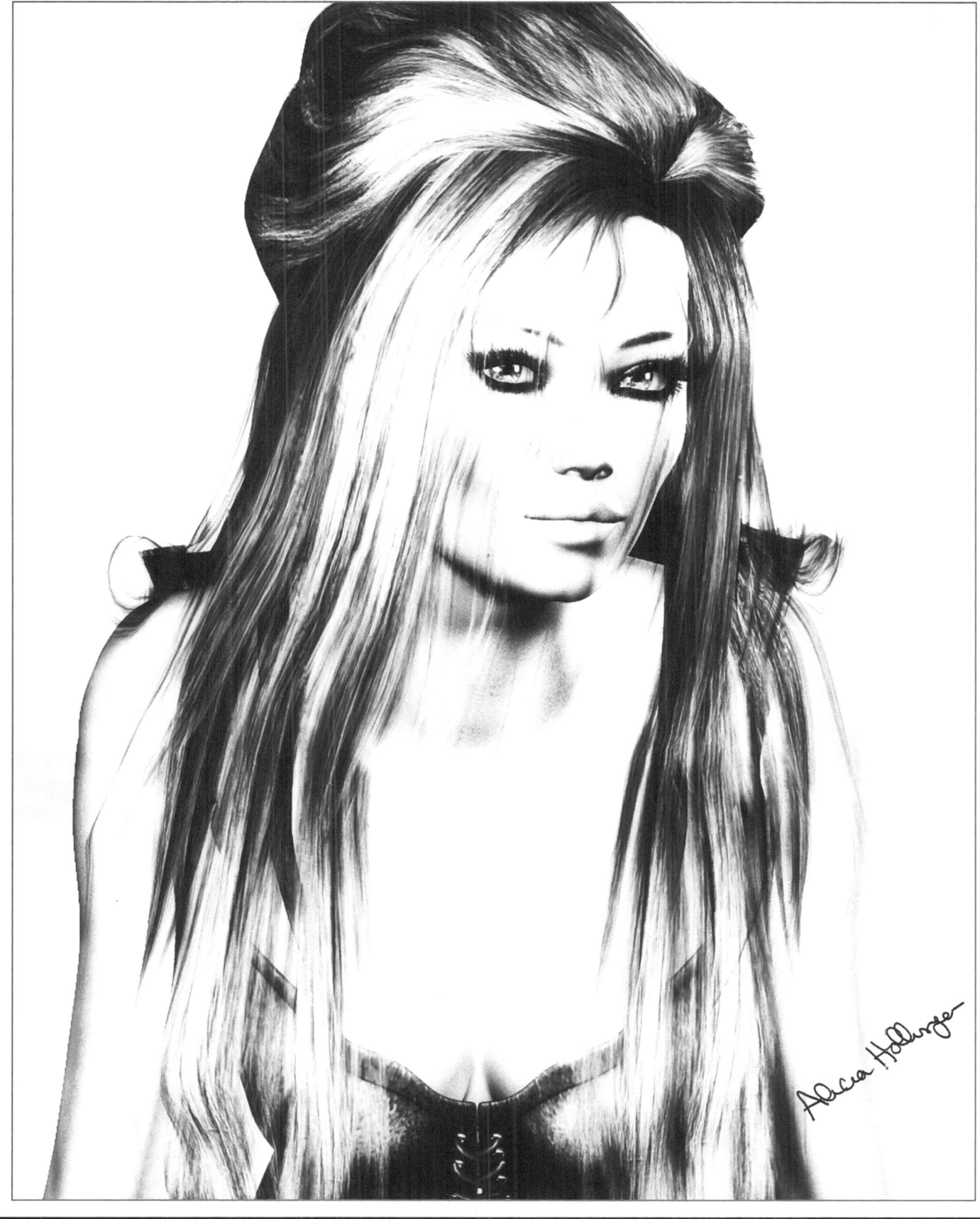

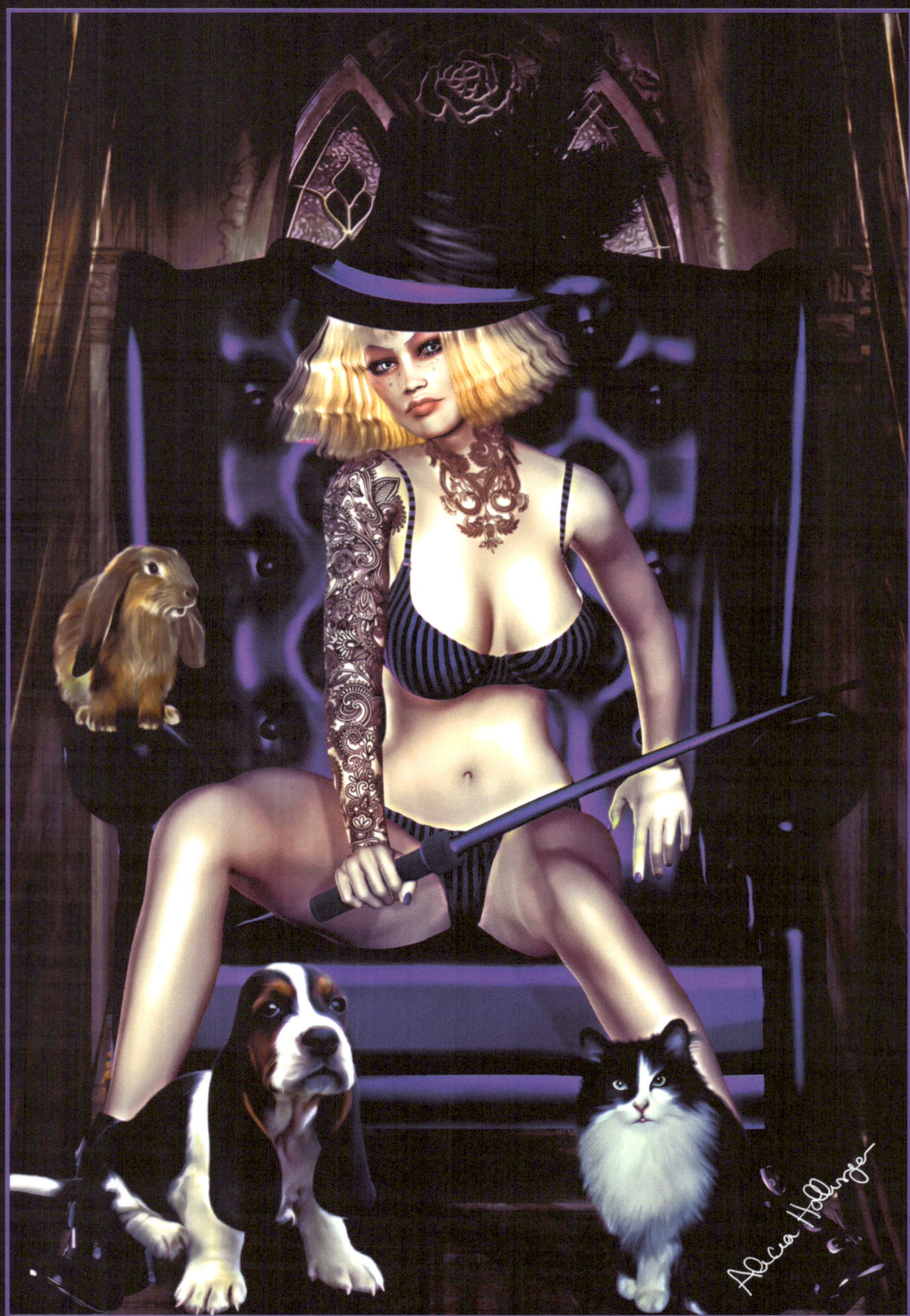

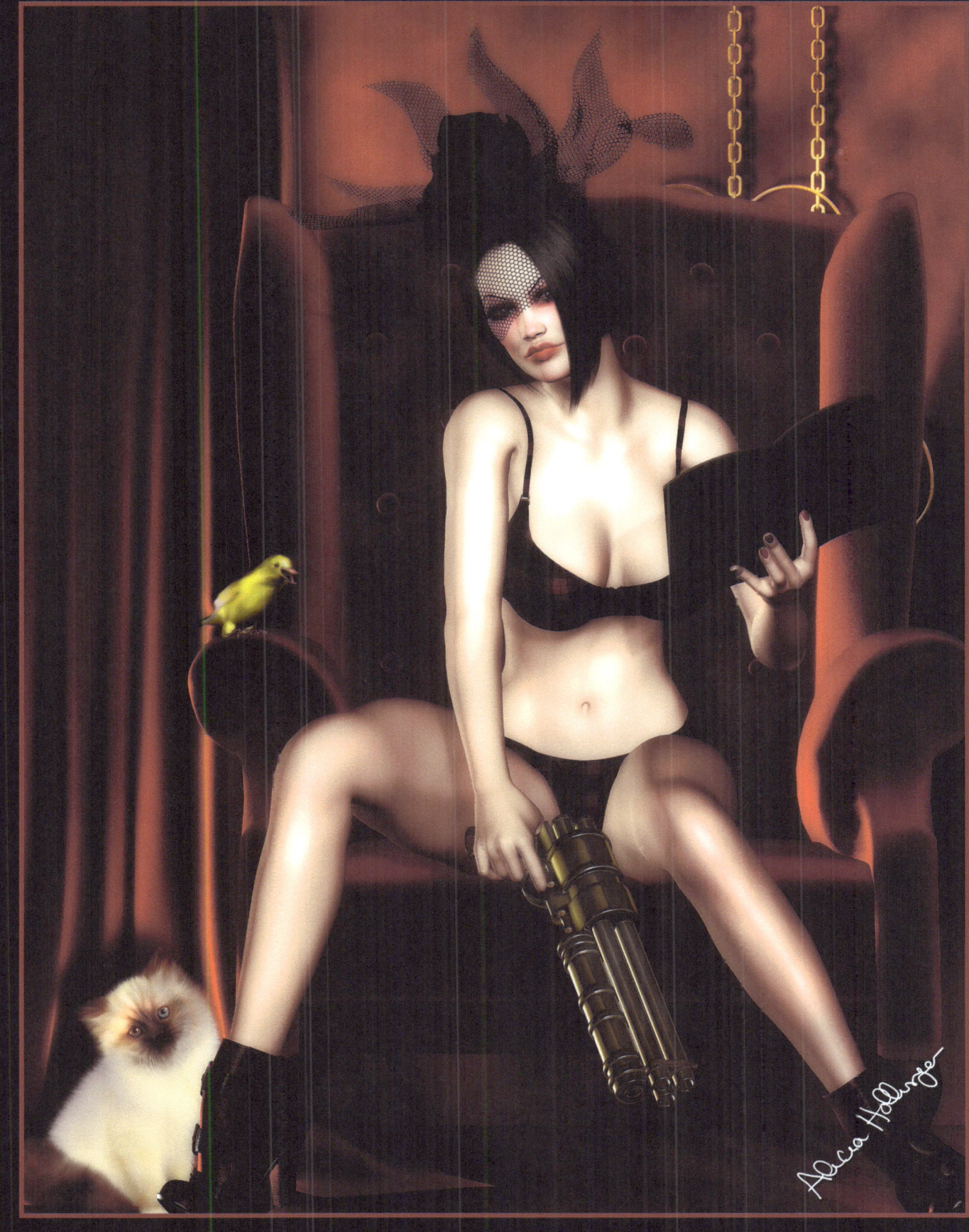

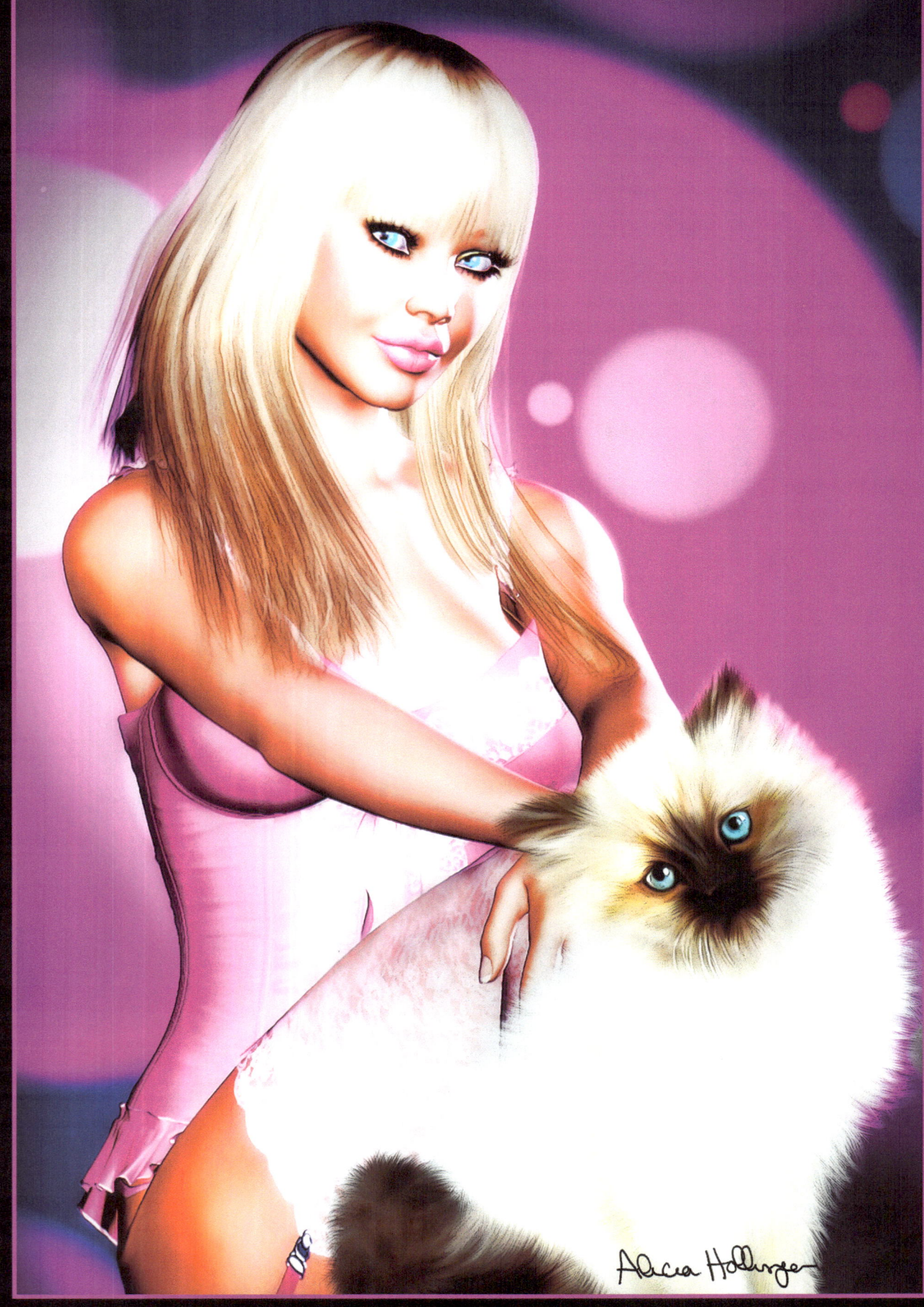

Alicia Hollinger

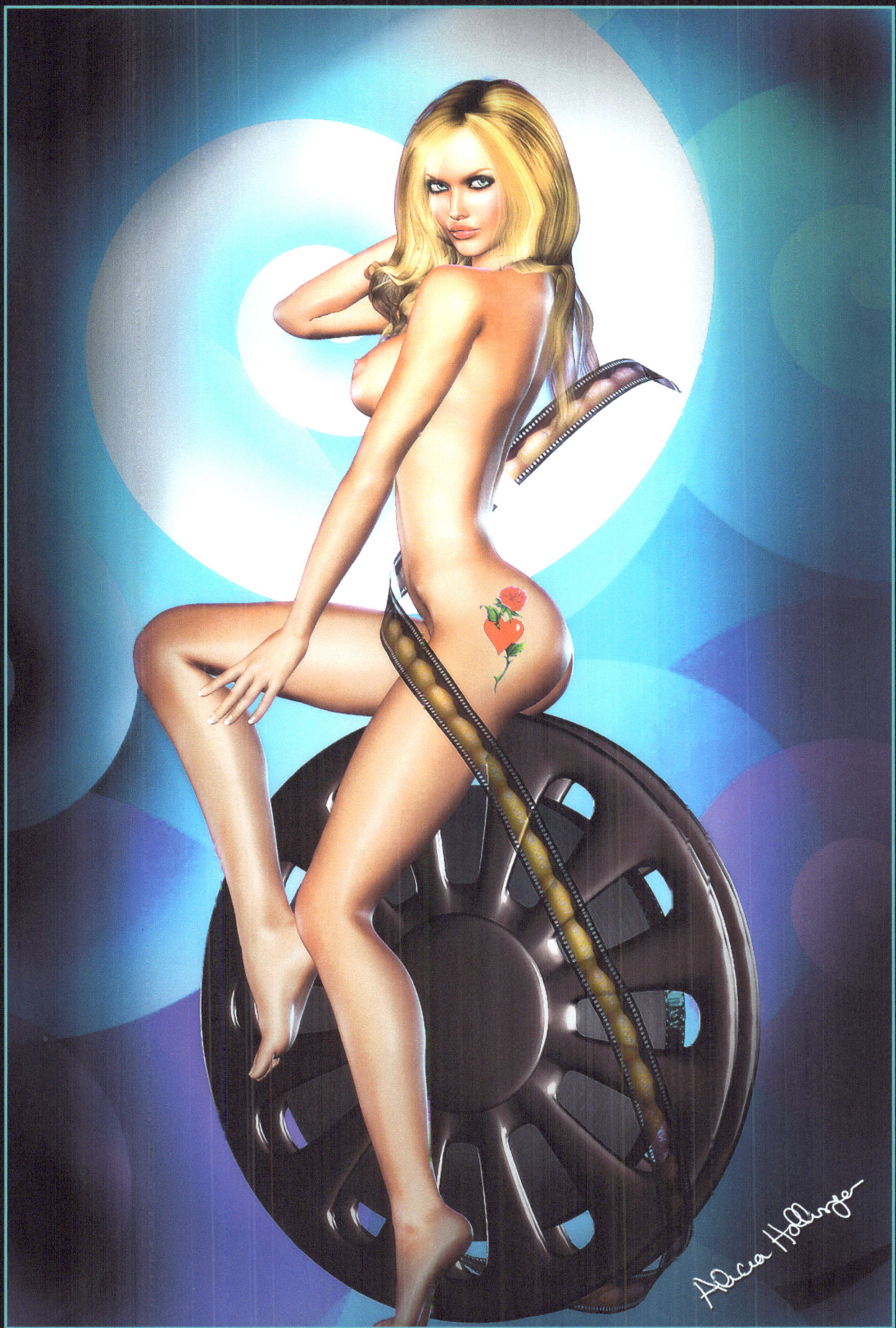

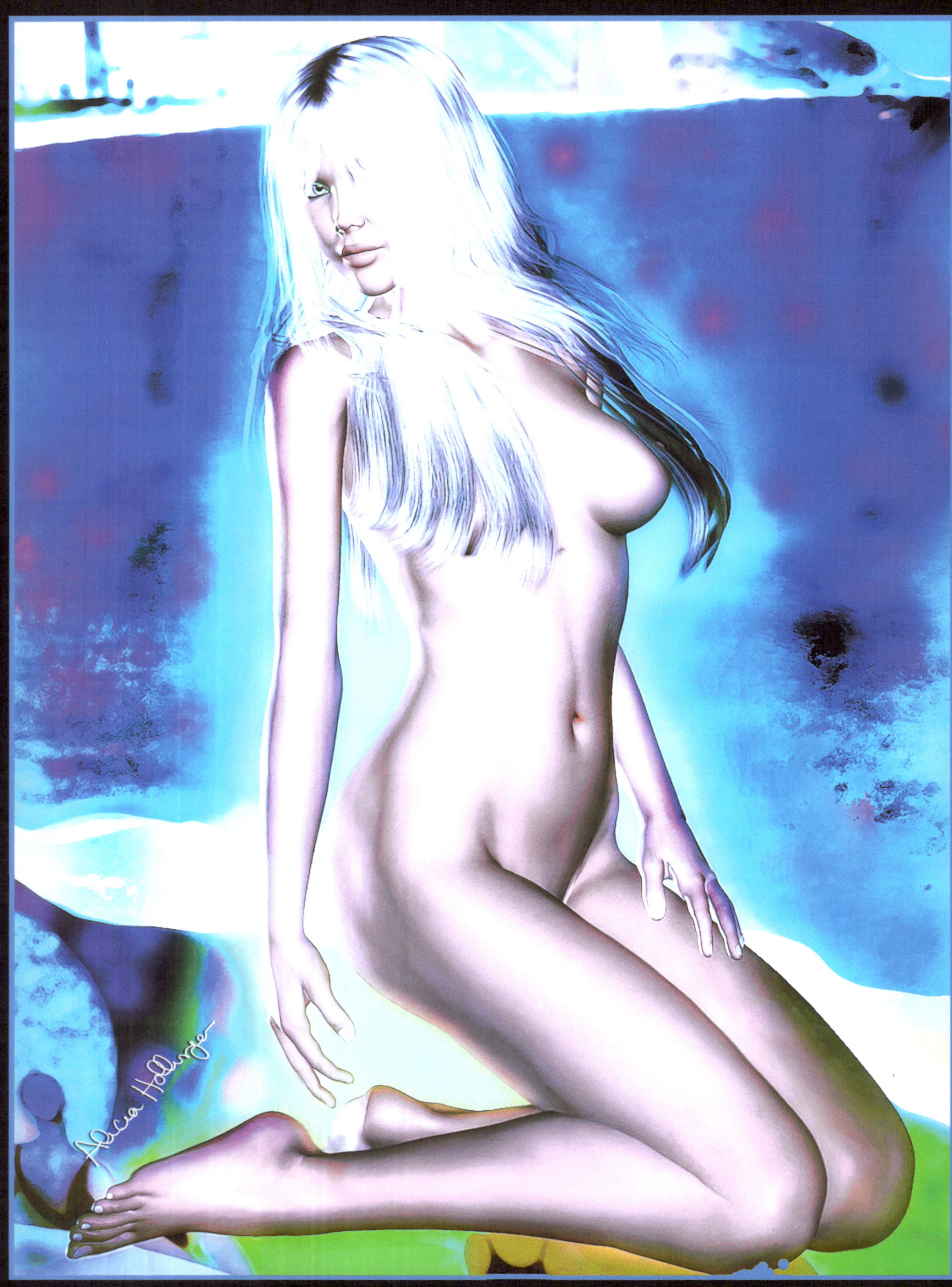

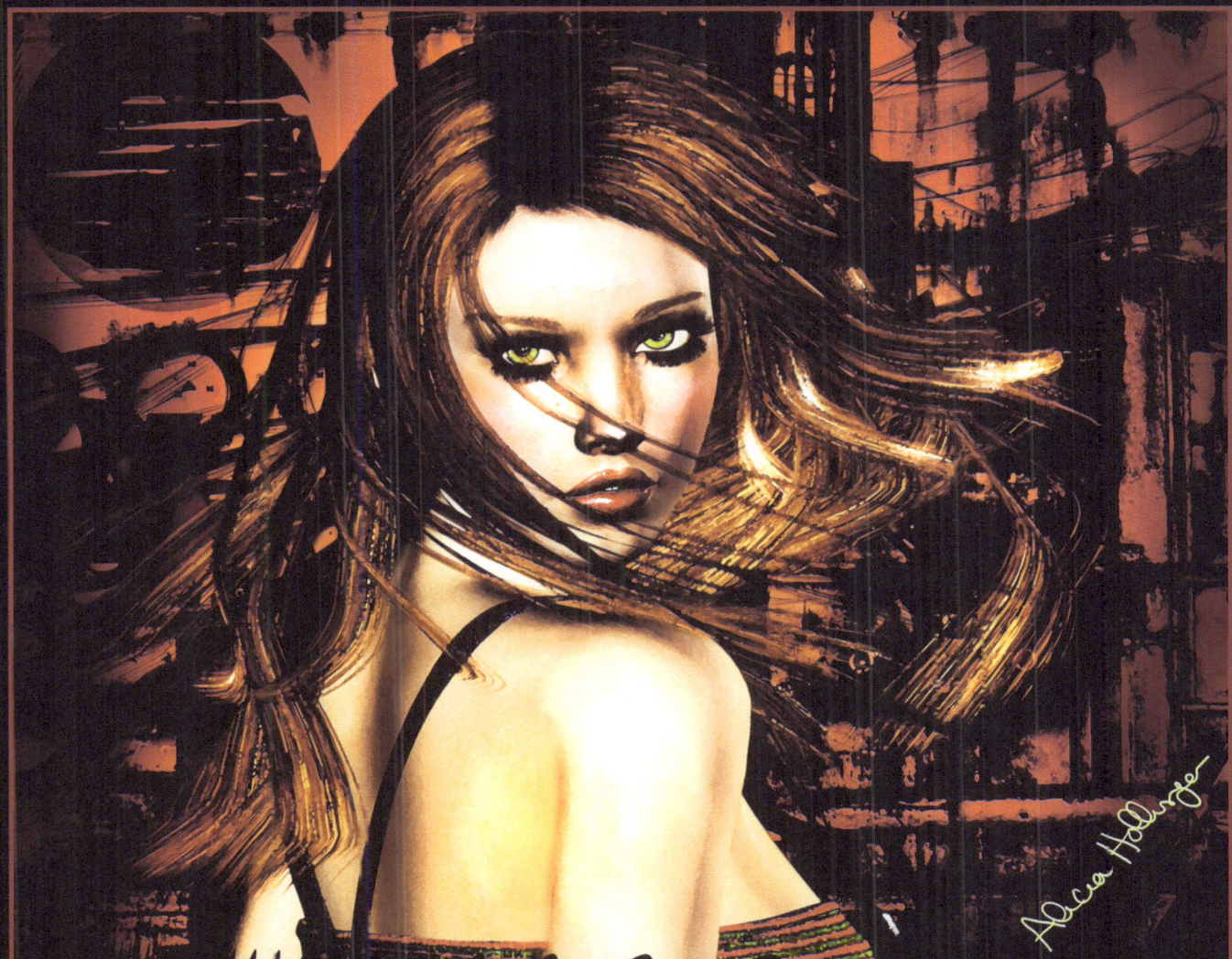

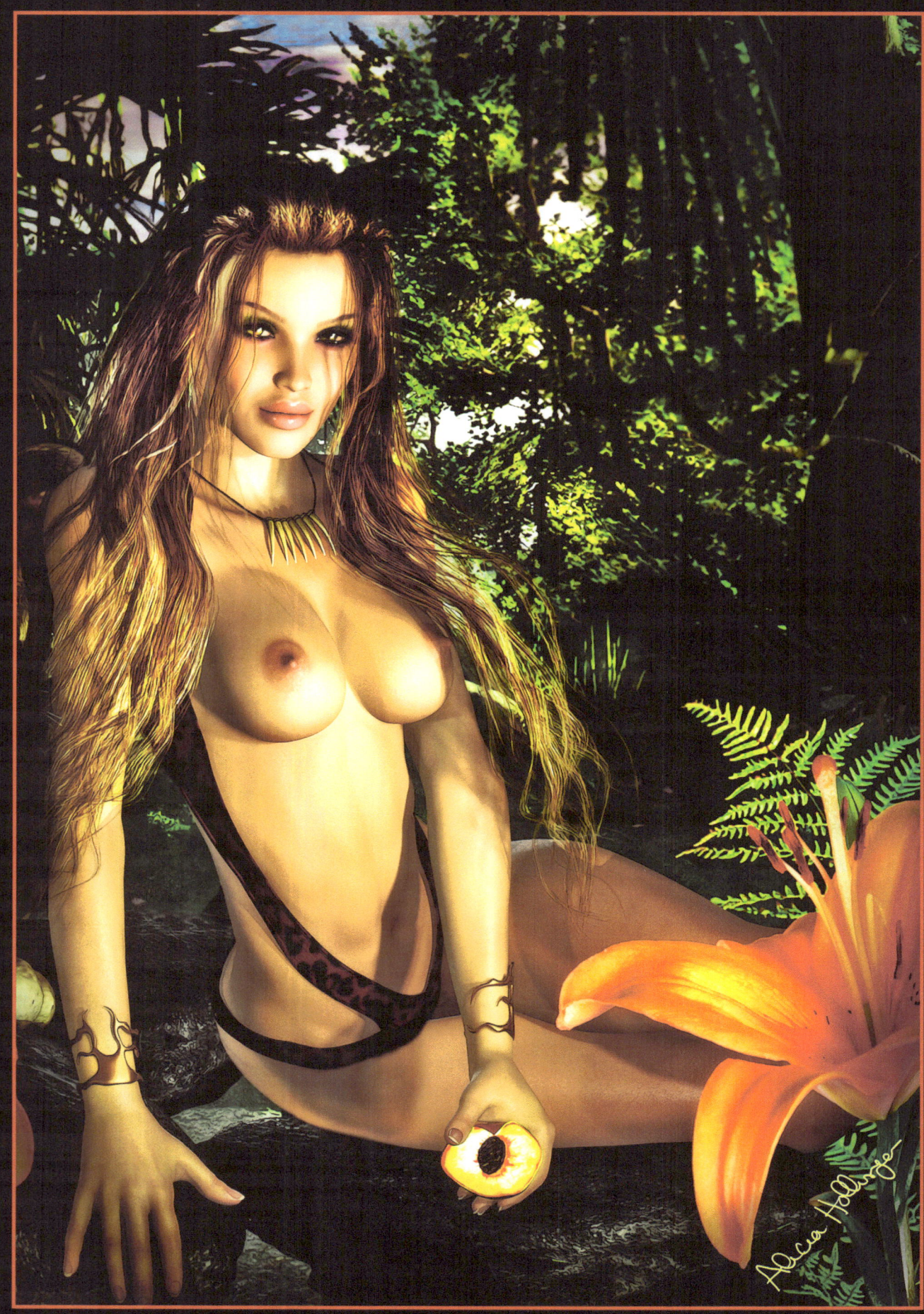

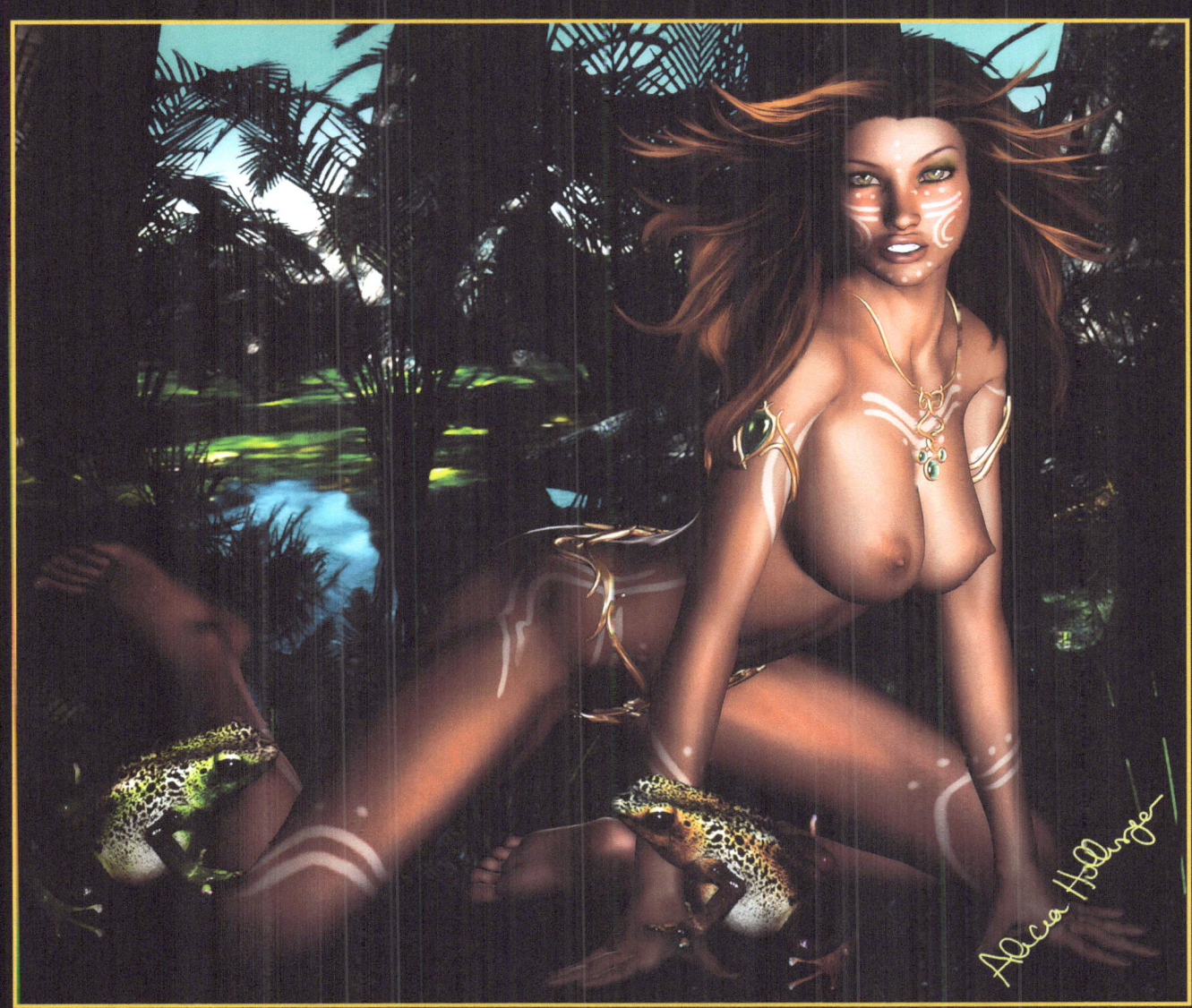

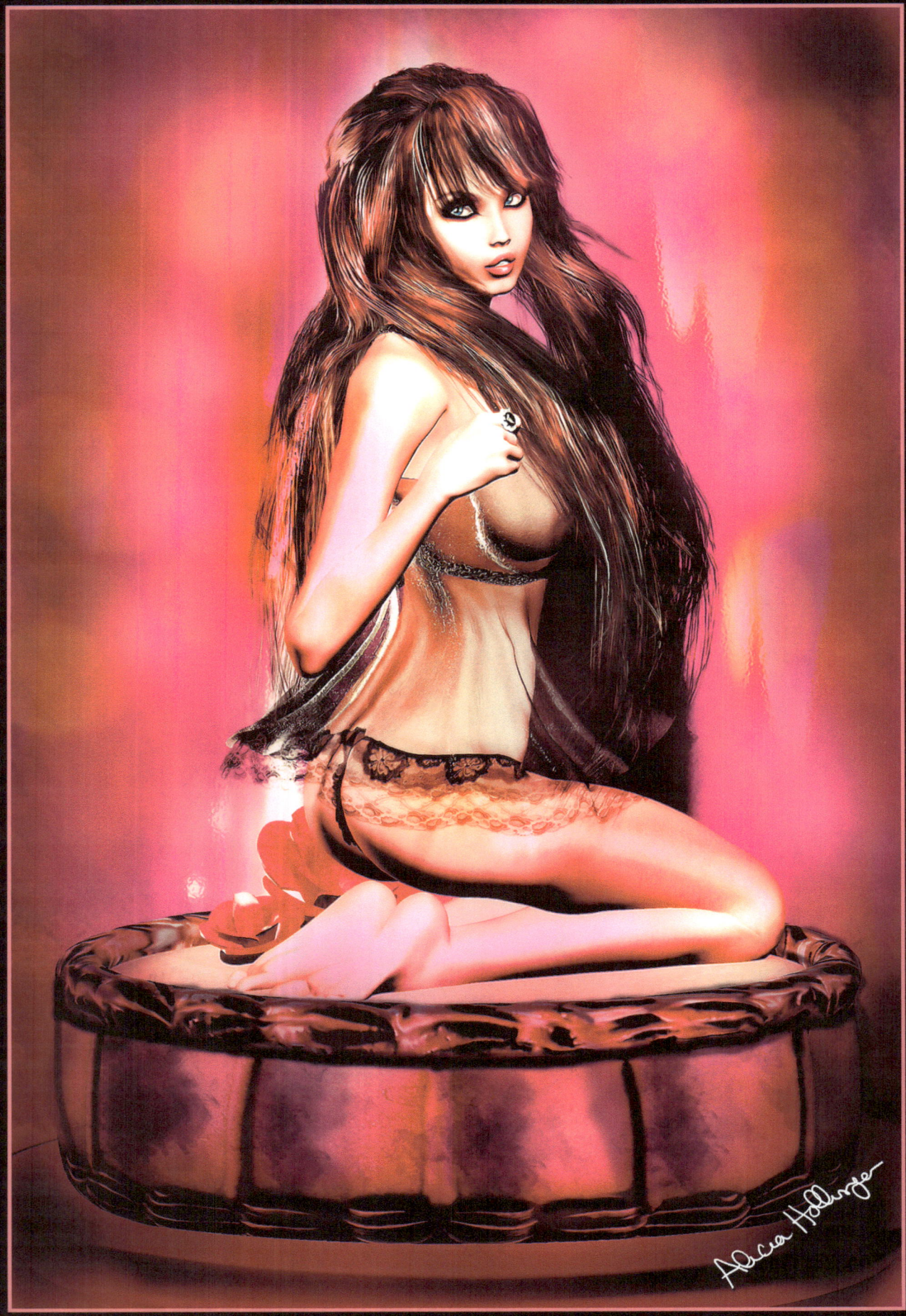

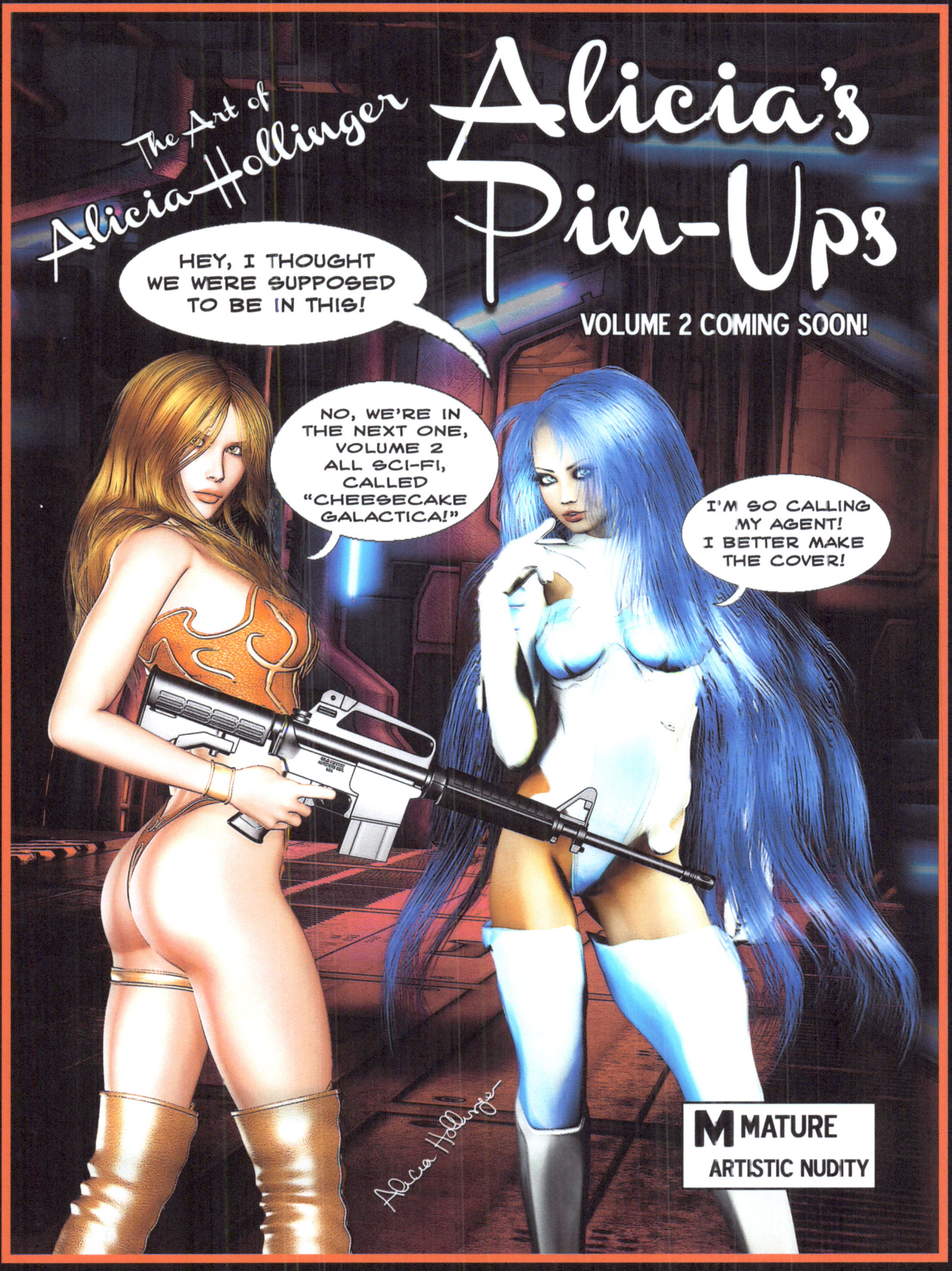
The Art of
Alicia Hollinger
Alicia's Pin-Ups
HEY, I THOUGHT WE WERE SUPPOSED TO BE IN THIS!
VOLUME 2 COMING SOON!
NO, WE'RE IN THE NEXT ONE, VOLUME 2 ALL SCI-FI, CALLED "CHEESECAKE GALACTICA!"
I'M SO CALLING MY AGENT! I BETTER MAKE THE COVER!
Alicia Hollinger
M MATURE
ARTISTIC NUDITY

ABOUT ALICIA HOLLINGER

Alicia Hollinger is a Los Angeles-based digital artist and writer. She has had a variety of careers, ranging from wannabe actress, film acquisitions/development/marketing/distribution executive, host for the Learning Annex, and Certified Hypnotherapist. She is also known as a bit of a socialite, attending parties and events in L.A., as well as at Cannes, Sundance, and various other film festivals, conventions, and pretty much any alluring festivity with an open bar. After attending Comic-Con in 2009, she began to focus her attention on creating sci-fi and fantasy pin-up art and moving forward with her writing.

Since she was a small child in her crib, Alicia had "lucid dreams," which allowed her to be aware that she was dreaming *while* she was dreaming that later sparked an interest in theoretical quantum physics and the nature of reality and has had a huge affect on the way she perceives the world. Her father would often admonish her for living in a "dreamworld," but she often wonders if life is just a dream… Row, row, row your boat gently down the stream… Luckily, living in a dreamworld is a good thing for art and writing, not so good if she had decided to become an accountant or a lawyer.

Alicia's digital art focuses on sexy pop culture pin-up art, sci-fi, fantasy, comic-book, video game, artistic, toon and realistic beautiful women, as well as children's art and sci-fi scenic art.

She has shown her art at Petra Gallery in Beverly Hills, Meltdown Comics Gallery in Hollywood, Pixeldrip Gallery events, Nucleus Gallery in Los Angeles, Titmouse Studios Hollywood, L.A.'s Comic Book Sunday, pop-up store galleries in LA, Long Beach Comic-Con, Wondercon, Condor-Con, LA Horror Fest, LA Pop-Con and Stan Lee's Comikaze. Her work has been featured in a book published by Heavy Metal Magazine, and she is currently working a pin-up digital comic book, more pin-up art books, a novelization of her screenplay and a sci-fi transmedia project.

Art prints in various sizes and commissions available. Also graphic design and CGI art (3D renders) for marketing, promotion, ads, websites, book, CD, DVD covers, games, movie one-sheets, etc...

FACEBOOK: http://www.facebook.com/AliciaHollingerArt
TWITTER: http://www.twitter.com/AliciaHollinger (@AliciaHollinger)
Contact: info@WonderlandArt.biz

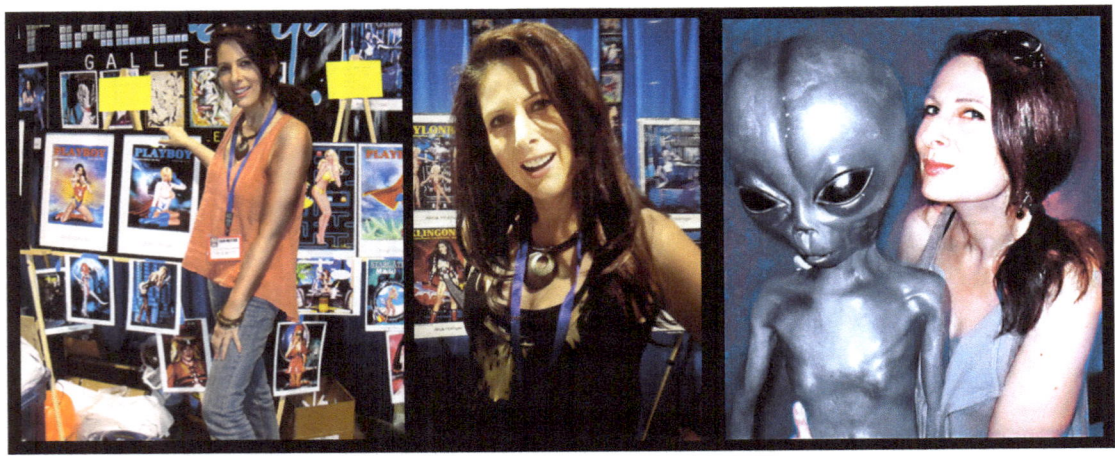